CRISES

AND

GROWTH

*Making the Most
of Hard Times*

Anita L. Spencer, Ph.D.

PAULIST PRESS / NEW YORK / MAHWAH

Book design by Ellen Whitney

Library of Congress Cataloging-in-Publication Data

Spencer, Anita Louise.
Crises and growth: making the most of hard times/by Anita L. Spencer.
p. cm.
Bibliography: p.
ISBN 0-8091-3013-0 (pbk.)
1. Christian life—Catholic authors.   I. Title.
BX2350.2.S593   1988
248.8'6—dc19
88-19048
CIP

Published by Paulist Press
997 Macarthur Boulevard
Mahwah, NJ 07430

Printed and bound in the
United States of America

Contents

Introduction

The subject matter of this book is not easy to talk about or to contemplate. No one likes to think of a crisis in personal terms. It should never happen to us—someone else, maybe, but certainly not us.

I used to really worry about such a thing happening to me when I was just a little girl. I grew up in the 1950's raised on stories of the saints. It was a time when Catholicism very much emphasized the saints as role models that we could all emulate. I heard stories about how various saints were tortured for their faith. These stories had a tremendous impact on me. They frightened me to death! I was so afraid that God would someday test me in the same way. I just knew that I would fail because I had a very low tolerance for pain. And all the saints that I had read about endured tremendous pain when their loyalty to God was put to the test.

I began to pray every day that God would never test me in such a way because I was sure that I could never bear such an experience. I used to console myself when my religion teachers told me that God never gives anyone a cross too big to bear. After hearing that, I reassured myself that I was therefore safe.

Such is the reasoning of a young child. I am many years older and wiser now and I have to say that many crises did come into my life after all. As a human being I am subject to the same reality as everyone else. And that reality is that we are all bound to experience setbacks, failures, losses and crises throughout our lives. This fact is unavoidable and universal because we are all human.

I wish that I could tell you that such experiences will never happen to you, just as I tried to convince myself that they would never happen to me—that we would never experience a crisis. But psychologists are in the business of telling the truth about life. And I have to say to you that no one escapes experiencing the inevitable losses of life (unless one dies very young).

Judith Viorst, author of the best-seller *Necessary Losses*, talks about the loves, illusions, dependencies and impossible expectations that all of us have to give up in order to grow. When we think of loss we usually think of the loss of a loved one through death. But Viorst tells us that loss is a far more encompassing theme in our lives. "For we lose not only through death, but also by leaving and being left, by changing and letting go and moving on. Our losses include not only our separations and departures from those we love, but our conscious and unconscious losses of romantic dreams, impossible expectations, illusions of freedom and power, illusions of safety—and the loss of our own younger self, the self that thought it always would be unwrinkled and invulnerable and immortal."[1]

Every crisis involves the potential for loss. It could be the loss of a relationship, loss of a career, loss of health, loss of status, etc. But it is my firm conviction and the premise of Viorst's book that we can learn immensely from our losses. It is through them that we grow and develop our full potential. It may well be that this particular loss or crisis we are experiencing was absolutely necessary in order to teach us a particular lesson about life. It may well be that we could not have learned that particular lesson in any other way. The challenge that any crisis entails results in the development of character. You gain strength from surviving such experiences.

When you think about it, there is really no more searching test of the human spirit than the way it behaves when fortune is adverse and it has to pass through a prolonged period of disappointing failures. Then comes the real proof of the person. "Achievement, if a man has the ability, is a joy; but to take hard knocks and come up smiling, to have your mainsail blown away and then rig a sheet on the bowsprit and sail on—this is perhaps the deepest test of character."[2]

I personally know a great deal about crisis and pain. My prayers could not protect me from such experiences. I can now tell you that I am very thankful that God did not answer my prayers because my pain has taught me so much. It is the crises I have experienced that have made me the person I am today. I now see that God does not permit any troubles to come upon us unless he has a specific plan by which great blessing can come out of the difficulty.

Having survived some very difficult times has given me the expertise to help many others during their personal journeys through darkness. This is because I have been "schooled in pain." It is precisely this education that was needed for my own personal growth and in order for me to become a credible psychologist. It is my belief that I can best help others if I have first been there myself.

I have gained many insights about how to survive crises from my own experiences and those of others. I have also researched what others have to say about this important subject. Perhaps what I have learned will be of some help to you.

We are all the "walking wounded," and it is these wounds that connect us all. "There are no rose gardens without thorns and those who would have nothing to do with thorns must never attempt to gather flowers."[3] In other words, you cannot have happiness without pain.

Until we hit enough pain, we will not be willing to deal with life's real issues. Pain is life's way of requiring that we face certain realities. We all have lessons to learn. It is my belief that if we don't learn them now, life will force us eventually into a position of such intense pain that we will be forced to learn them. Every crisis is really a challenge and can be a tremendous learning experience.

This is a book about crises and how to take these inevitable experiences and use them as catalysts for growth and change. We can discover newfound strength and character as we learn to weather life's storms. No matter what happens to us, we can discover that we are survivors and can go on to be much more than we ever thought possible.

The endurance of the human spirit is truly amazing, and I have always believed that resiliency is a very important factor in living. "The winds of life may bind us, but if we have resilience of spirit, they cannot break us. To have the capacity to courageously straighten again after our heads have been bowed by defeat, disappointment and suffering is the supreme test of character."[4]

Life can be looked on as a school with certain lessons that must be learned. If we allow ourselves to learn these lessons well, we will discover that growing, changing and becoming is really what life is all about. It is my hope that this book will in some way help you in this process.

Chapter 1

—— • ——

What Is a Crisis?

The term crisis is derived from the Greek word *krisis*, which means decision or turning point. A crisis occurs when a person faces an obstacle to important life goals that is, for a time, insurmountable through the utilization of customary methods of problem solving. A period of disorganization ensues, a period of upset, during which many abortive attempts at solution are made.

According to Gerald Caplan, a crisis is a transitional period or turning point in life. On the one hand, it presents the individual concerned with the opportunity for acquiring greater mastery and for achieving personality growth; on the other hand, there is the risk of increased vulnerability and mental breakdown. A crisis is the experience of being confronted with an unfamiliar obstacle in life's path. The familiar resources and past experience of the individual come under test and may be found wanting. A crisis can therefore present a challenge to customary habits and, if successfully met, become a stimulus to fruitful innovation and further development. If an individual's customary methods of problem-solving fail and inadequate or inappropriate help has been received in meeting the impasse, he or she may become disorganized and may develop an acute anxiety state, depression, or other disabling disorders.[1]

What is critical to understand about a crisis is that the person experiencing it is normally in a state of relative equilibrium or emotional balance and has a repertoire of problem-solving skills. But now a hazardous event or an obstacle to a goal cannot be overcome by the usual problem-solving or coping skills. This lack of fit between the event and the skills proves disorganizing and disrupting for the person, and anxiety increases. With the increase in anxiety, the coping powers further decrease.

Furthermore, a crisis is an individual matter. What may be a crisis for one person may not be a crisis for another, or, for that matter, may not have been a crisis for the same person at some other time. Many kinds of events have the potential to be a crisis—the death of a loved one, separation from a significant other, divorce, unwanted pregnancy, rape, bankruptcy, flood, earthquake, fire, illness, etc. Even positive events can cause us problems due to added stress that is associated with them—moving to a new residence, marriage, birth of a baby, graduation, retirement, etc. Any given event may have the potential to create demands beyond one's coping abilities.

There are two categories of crisis: the expected, developmental, maturational crises that occur as a person grows and develops, and the unexpected, accidental, situational crises that are not anticipated.

Type I Crisis

This first type of crisis is considered to be developmental due to the fact that throughout the various stages and ages of life, physical, psychological, and environmental shifts are likely to occur. Comparable crises occur with each developmental stage.

Each developmental stage usually begins with a transition period. We have all heard of the term "midlife crisis" or the "identity crisis" of adolescence. These are good examples of transition periods. In every transition we must reappraise what we have done in the past and make some choices about what we want for the future. We can make drastic changes or make less obvious ones, but some change is necessary if we are to evolve and grow. If we don't grow we stagnate, and life becomes empty and meaningless as a result.

A transition can be a very fulfilling time if we allow ourselves to discover new facets of our personality and find new opportunities to develop our potential. But it can be a time of despair and bitterness if we only look at the passage of time as something negative. If we only value ourselves in terms of qualities attributed to youth, we will not see the opportunities that each stage of life offers.

The problem with developmental crises is that they involve life changes. And all major life changes are potentially stressful. The process begins with birth and is followed by well documented stages through childhood. A pattern begins to develop—stable periods alternate with passages in between, all through adulthood. (See, for example, Gail Sheehey's *Passages*, Daniel Levinson's *Seasons of a Man's Life*, or my book *Seasons: A Woman's Search for Self Through Life's Stages*.)

Even a major change that is anticipated and generally thought desirable (such as leaving home or getting married) demands letting go of a familiar, protective identity, and that is always a risk. We don't know if the change will be for the better. This fact worries us and results in our feeling very vulnerable. We are uncertain about ourselves. Maybe the change won't work out. But it is from this anxiety and stress that we are able to gather the necessary strength and energy to go through the change. In the process, we discover within ourselves an increased awareness. This gives us the hope that the change will be positive.

The goal of personality development is the achievement of individuation. This term was coined by Carl Jung and means that the person has developed all aspects of his or her personality. A person who is undergoing the individuation process is consciously realizing and integrating all of one's possibilities. Individuation is self-realization.

The individuation process cannot be grasped in its deepest essence because it is a part of the mystery of transformation that pervades all creation. It includes within it the secret of life, which is ceaselessly reborn in passing through an ever renewed "death."[2]

Jung states that if people are to live, they must fight and sacrifice their longing for the past in order to rise to their own heights. And having reached the noonday heights, they must sacrifice their love for their own achievement, for they may not loiter. "The sun, too, sacrifices its greatest strength in order to hasten onward to the fruits of autumn, which are the seeds of rebirth. If this sacrifice is made willingly—a deed possible for man alone and demanded again and again on the way of individuation—transformation and rebirth ensue."[3]

Jolande Jacobi sees the individuation process as involving four births. The first birth occurs when the bodily man or woman comes into life from the womb of the mother. The second occurs at puberty when the ego emancipates itself from its psychic fusion with the parental authority and acquires clearly defined form, independence, and sense of responsibility. The third birth occurs when the "spiritual body" emerges from the conflicts of middle life and, anchored again in the depths of the psyche, knowingly allies itself with the Self. Expressed in religious language, this experience is a "rebirth." The fourth birth takes place when the individual departs through the door of life and reenters the vast, unexplored land beyond death, from whence he or she came.[4]

Any person who does not allow individuation to take place and thereby interferes with this developmental process is doomed to live an unhealthy and unfulfilled life. Not following one's destiny, or trying to avoid one's fate, is a frequent cause of numerous psychic difficulties. Jacobi believes that the steady increase in the number of neurotics today is due to the fact that more and more individuals are called upon to work for their psychic wholeness, but that fewer and fewer of them are ready to do so. And any obstruction of the natural process of development or any avoidance of the law of life, or getting stuck on a level unsuited to one's age, takes its revenge. It may not be immediately; it could be later at the onset of the second half of life, in the form of serious crises, nervous breakdowns, and all manner of physical and psychic sufferings.[5]

Sometimes these people show up in a therapist's office experiencing certain symptoms. They are feeling guilty but they don't understand why. They know that they are not guilty of any bad deed, they have not given way to any illicit impulse, and yet they are plagued by uncertainty, discontent, despair, and above all by anxiety—a constant, indefinable anxiety. The truth is that they *are* guilty. Their guilt does not lie in the fact that they have a neurosis, but in the fact that, knowing they have one, they do nothing to set about curing it.[6]

What makes change so difficult is the fact that there is no change without pain. One cannot develop a new set of functional behaviors or attitudes without giving up anything. Neurotic behavior has its benefits, and this is why one holds on to it so desperately. Neurotic people believe that they need to maintain their self-defeating patterns in order to allay the dread of greater terrors or anxieties.

Every change is threatening because it requires us to surrender something that we have viewed as vital. Any change demands that we give up something, and therefore some degree of discomfort accompanies all new behavior. Any illusion of painless change creates additional disappointment when the real cost of self-improvement becomes apparent.

It is extremely important to allow oneself to submit to this individuation process. It is not only a way of developing one's own nature, but a psychotherapeutic necessity for all who suffer from afflictions of the soul. Developmental crises are extremely important and must be addressed so that the necessary psychic changes appropriate for the next stage of life are allowed to occur.

Type II Crisis

This second type of crisis is the unexpected, accidental, situational crisis that is not anticipated. Examples of this type are the birth of a premature baby, death of a loved one, loss of a job, unanticipated divorce, loss of a body part or body function, etc. In each of these examples, the person is progressing through life in a steady state or in relative emotional balance when the occurrence of the event presents the stimulus for a change reaction and a period of disequilibrium.

Losses such as these change us and our life course. The unavoidable reality is that one can never be the same. There is often great sorrow in this reality. Even if we wished to remain the persons we previously were, it is simply not possible. Our lives may be permanently damaged by a crisis or permanently strengthened. Each situation is unique, and only we ourselves can search the answers concerning the changed life and self that will emerge.

Many times the occurrence of an unexpected Type II crisis forces us to face the fact that we have not worked through previous developmental Type I crises. Because developmental crises can often be ignored if the symptoms of distress are not too severe, we fail to grow. This fact comes back to haunt us when we are faced with accidental crises and find we do not have the necessary coping skills available.

As you will recall, individuation is the result of successfully resolving earlier developmental crises and thereby developing and integrating more aspects of the personality. The resultant new-found strength and flexibility will be very much needed when we are forced to face the kinds of very painful situations that Type II crises entail.

It is imperative that we develop our potential and gain the self-knowledge necessary to travel through life. Type I developmental crises help us do just that. The resolution of a Type II crisis has as a prerequisite that we have successfully navigated Type I crises. The following story well illustrates this point.

There is a Buddhist parable about a young prince who completes his military studies under a renowned teacher and is accorded the title of "Prince Five-Weapons" for his distinction, and armed with the five weapons so mentioned, he sets out on the road leading to the city of his father, the king.

On the way he comes to a forest. People at the mouth of the forest warn him not to enter the forest, telling him an ogre lives there named "Sticky-Hair" who kills every man he sees. The young prince, confident in his training and hence fearless, enters the forest and in due time meets the ogre who engages him in battle. Each of the prince's weapons is soon rendered useless as the ogre, whose head is as big as a summer house, deflects each of them with his hair and they stick there. But after each weapon is immobilized, the prince challenges the ogre again and finally the ogre says to him:

"Youth, why are you not afraid?"

"Ogre," the prince answers, "why should I be afraid? For in one's life one's death is absolutely certain. What's more, I have in my belly a thunderbolt for a weapon."

And the ogre, understanding the weapon that the prince referred to as a thunderbolt was the Weapon of Self-Knowledge within him, let him go immediately, and the prince walked out of the forest a free man.[7]

This story reminds us of the importance of working on ourselves throughout the life cycle so that we will be better prepared for life. We need to remember that life is a school with many lessons to learn. We won't be able to survive very well as adults if we refuse to attend this school and learn its lessons to the best of our ability.

Characteristics of a Crisis

According to Robert Veninga, there are six common characteristics of a crisis. These characteristics are more pertinent for Type II crises—unexpected, accidental or situational crises. But they may also occur in some developmental crises (Type I crisis). They are as follows:

1. A crisis hits suddenly, without warning.

2. A crisis threatens security.

3. The resolution of a crisis is unpredictable. We don't know how things will turn out.

4. A crisis presents dilemmas. This is because there are no clear-cut solutions to difficult problems. Sometimes you will be forced to make decisions on little information.

5. A crisis erodes self-confidence. You lose your confidence and begin to approach life with apprehension. The sudden impact of a negative event reminds us that life is fragile.

6. A difficult experience helps us redefine our values. Jean-Paul Sartre states that you cannot understand "being" (life) until you comprehend "non-being" (death). For when one stares death squarely in the face, then one begins to comprehend the profound gifts of life. In the midst of tragedy, we learn what is important, and that is the redemptive legacy of any crisis experience.[8]

In addition to the six characteristics of a crisis mentioned above, there are some additional attributes of crises that are important to mention. Again, these characteristics are more applicable to Type II crises. These attributes have been discovered by professionals who deal with people and families in crisis.

1. Crises are self-limiting in time. Some resolution to a crisis will occur within four to six weeks of the precipitating trauma, though the outcome may vary greatly in adaptiveness from a reality-oriented solution of the problem to a maladaptive solution which leads on to chronic dysfunction. The situation may be complicated by the appearance of multiple hazards, the

later hazards sometimes resulting from the maladaptive resolution of the initial crisis.

2. Dependency needs are invariably expressed in the early stages of crisis, though their expression may be indirect. There may be open and direct requests for help to family and friends. Sometimes the expressions of need may be disguised and the individual becomes distressed or develops physical symptoms. Attention may be drawn to the individual's crisis by a deterioration of effectiveness at work or in the home. Distress may be signaled by children in disturbed or disruptive behavior. This is oftentimes a child's way of crying out for help.

3. Individual crisis may be symptomatic of a crisis within the family which occurs when their collective coping resources fail to overcome a problem facing all of them. In this event, one member may manifest the features of crisis for the whole family. The individual with the current crisis may be, quite simply, the most vulnerable psychologically. Sometimes one individual is chosen to carry the burden of crisis for the whole family, either because of some symbolic position held within the family or because the individual is the usual scapegoat for all problems.

4. Crisis is not, in itself, a pathological state, though its outcome might be. Crisis presents the opportunity for personality growth if a constructive resolution is achieved. The individual who successfully masters a crisis learns new methods of coping, and in the process learns something valuable. The family which successfully negotiates a crisis often achieves a new flexibility and closeness.

5. Crisis presents the opportunity for resolution of old conflicts, derived from the maladaptive solution of earlier crises. It is characteristic of crisis that unresolved, unconscious conflicts are reactivated, often accompanied by the appropriate feeling state. The danger is that past maladaptive patterns of problem solving will be repeated in the present crisis.

It is my belief that attribute #5 is a very important one. Crisis is an opportunity. My favorite definition of crisis comes from the ancient Chinese. They define crisis as an opportunity riding on dangerous winds. In other words, crisis is both frightening and exciting. You can't run away from it—there is simply no place to run. Life forces you to make choices and changes. As Gail Sheehy states in her book *Pathfinders*, "All of us, at some time in our life, have stood at a crossroad where two roads diverged and doubted our wisdom to choose. Many of us have chosen by refusing to risk moving at all. Others of us have made a choice by default or been unaware even that we stood at a crossroad. But some among us have recognized that crossroad and seen in it the path to another beginning, an opportunity to make ourselves more."[9]

When it comes right down to it, what is really important is not so much what happens to us but *how we take it*. Do we benefit from the experience? It is my belief that crisis can show us the truth in the words: "That which does not kill you, makes you stronger." My work has convinced me that we can accept the basic script handed down to us at birth and play it out, passively, actively or bitterly. Or we can intervene consciously in the process and risk making changes in our lives. Let's face it, life involves a great deal of risk. There are numerous obstacles that must be overcome. Life becomes a journey that we can either choose or not choose to take. By learning to view crises as opportunities we take a more positive approach to this journey. The question is, "How can we best use this opportunity?"

Chapter 2

---•---

Crisis as an Opportunity

One way or another, a crisis is likely to be resolved within two months after the occurrence of the precipitating event. The resolution can lead to a lifestyle that is more, less, or equally effective in comparison to the pre-crisis state. Traditional life patterns that prove ineffective in resolving a crisis may be discarded in favor of new approaches that alleviate the stress. After the turmoil has subsided, the person's life may be quite different from the way it was before a crisis. A crisis may be a call to new action. Its challenge may elicit new coping mechanisms, new behavior, and, consequently, a higher level of mental health.

Years later, most people, as they look back on a particularly difficult period in their life, will readily admit that some good came out of it. And in spite of the anger, the bitterness, even the self-doubts, they were able to move into a new stage in their lives. No one has to be a victim, no matter how terrible the loss. Something new can be learned about ourselves and about life from even the most painful losses.

One of my favorite quotes comes from Viktor Frankl. He tells us that "everything precious including our dignity can be taken from us but the one thing that cannot be taken away is our power to choose what attitude we will take toward the events that have happened."[1] In other words, it is possible for all of us to find the courage to survive and transform something very painful into something positive.

I have a plaque on my office wall that says "When life gives you lemons, make lemonade." I have this on my wall to constantly remind me of this truth. Another favorite motto of mine is "Life is God's gift to you; what you do with your life is your gift to God." I have tried to model my life after both of these wise truths. I view crisis as a challenge and see it as a catalyst for tremendous growth and change. Loss can be a stop point or a pause point. It can be a coffin or a catapult. We make the choice about which it will be. God offers us the challenge to grow and achieve our potential—to be all that we can be. He will give us the strength to overcome. He offers comfort and support to all of us—the walking wounded.

Learning from Life

A number of years ago I went through a very unexpected and difficult divorce. It was a very devastating experience for me and one I was sure would never happen. I am a very sensitive individual and have always tried very hard to do my best in everything. I used to pray to God every night that he would help me be a better person. But not even being a better person was going to stop that divorce. I felt very powerless and very out of control. This experience made me realize that the only thing that I had any control over was my actions in response to this crisis. I made up my mind that no matter what else happened I would not waste this opportunity. I would find some way of transforming this crisis. *That* I did have the power to do. I knew there must be some new lessons for me to learn. I also knew that God would give me the strength to survive this crisis and, in some way, benefit from it.

My divorce occurred at a time when there were very few resources available to divorced, separated and widowed women. I, like many others, was not prepared to enter the working world. I had spent the bulk of my adult life raising children, never thinking I would need to someday support myself. Because of the lack of supportive services for women, I decided to create a program for displaced homemakers. I believed that I could use my own personal experiences in helping other women who were going through the same thing. By so doing, I could create something positive out of a very traumatic and negative experience.

I got the opportunity to create this program at the YWCA. In 1980 we opened the doors to women who were recently separated, divorced, or widowed, who faced an uncertain future and needed to make changes in their lives as a result. The major thrust of this program was to support women through this major crisis and help them create a new dream for themselves and their children.

It was my belief that this crisis could be used to help these women grow and to develop new parts of their personality never before utilized. I did not want to see them waste this opportunity. The loss of a spouse through divorce or death is one of the most stressful life changes a person can experience. Like any other of life's crises, it is to be avoided if possible, but when it occurs, it can be dealt with as a means of achieving growth toward a more satisfying way of life.

In order to best help these women, I wanted to base the program on sound psychological principles. I wanted to find a way to take the turmoil and confusion that already exists in the crisis state and use this to an advantage. During a a time of crisis it is easier to engage in creative problem solving because the person is much more flexible. Emotions, such as anger, can be a source of immense energy that can be utilized in making productive and necessary changes in a person's life.

Having this in mind, I decided to base the program on a theoretical model that would allow participants to optimize this crisis and turn it into a catalyst for growth and change. I believe this model can be used by anyone undergoing a crisis and is an excellent way to take a very negative experience and grow.

It is my conviction that there are tasks which must be accomplished in order for a person to recover from a crisis. Erik Erikson's developmental theories offer an excellent conceptual framework for viewing this process. His "stages of man" provide a framework through which to view the tasks of recovery from a crisis.

It is my belief that a positive recovery from a crisis will be the result if we allow ourselves to use this stressful time to reexperience some earlier inadequately worked through developmental issues. In other words, we want to eventually become like Prince Five-Weapons in the Buddhist parable mentioned in Chapter 1. We want to take this current crisis and use it to our advantage. We want to take this opportunity to work on those developmental issues that we have not previously resolved adequately. By doing so, we will be better armed, like Prince Five-Weapons, for all those future, unexpected crises that will inevitably occur.

I can readily admit today that my divorce forced me to deal with developmental issues that I had ignored. I had not developed the self-knowledge as had Prince Five-Weapons, and when this unexpected crisis hit I was quite unprepared. I was just about devoured by the ogre Sticky-Hair. This experience made me adopt the old adage "Fool me once, shame on you! Fool me twice, shame on me!" I was bound and determined to learn from my experience. I found my own way to do just that which I will gladly share with you.

A Theory for Change

The psychological theory that made the most sense to me and which I used in my program for displaced homemakers was one developed by Erik Erikson. This model can certainly be generalized and therefore used by any person undergoing a crisis. It helped me personally and helped many women going through my program and can be of help to you as well.

What Erikson did was to divide the whole life cycle into eight stages. Freud did something similar but ended his stages at adolescence with the assumption that psychosexual development ended there. But Erikson believed that growth takes place throughout the life cycle, to the day we die.

According to Erikson, the life cycle of the individual can be divided into eight stages. Throughout life, the individual faces crises that must be resolved in order for the personality to continue to develop. Each of Erikson's stages involves the solving of a particular life crisis.

An important concept to understand is that none of these eight stages or crises is ever resolved completely, only more so or less depending on the individual. Since each of Erikson's stages is built upon the previous stage, the person who more adequately solves an earlier crisis has a more stable foundation upon which to build.

Each stage of life, unfolding as it does in accordance with a definite and at least partially inborn ground plan, presents its own distinctive challenge to the individual. Erikson describes these challenges as normative crises or nuclear conflicts and asserts that there are eight of them to be resolved between birth and death. However, just as no person can ever be completely "gratified" or utterly "anxiety free," no one can ever resolve a nuclear conflict "once and for all." It is instead a matter of tipping the balance more in one direction than in another. Consequently, each conflict or crisis leaves its mark upon the individual.

In any crisis of major proportions it stands to reason that each of Erikson's stages is reactivated by the trauma. The unresolved parts of previous crises are reactivated and must be resolved in terms of the present crisis. Also, since more can be accomplished during a time of crisis when the usual defenses are shaken, there is a greater likelihood that the pain of the situation will provoke enough anxiety for a normal individual to gain insight and to grow.

The adequacy of the resolution of previous crises will determine the extent to which difficulties are presented by the unresolved issues at each developmental level. When previous stages were managed poorly—that is, a crisis was not resolved successfully—the current crisis may activate larger problems than when the previous solutions were adequate. Prince Five-Weapons had obviously done his homework and worked on relevant developmental issues or he never would have been strong enough to meet the challenge of the ogre Sticky-Hair.

Each of Erikson's eight stages is applicable when experiencing a crisis and offers us an opportunity to work on inadequately resolved developmental issues. I attempted to do some further psychological work on these issues when I was in the midst of my divorce crisis. I set up the displaced homemakers' program in such a way that each woman would also have an opportunity to do some further work on these developmental issues. Erikson's eight stages and a method for addressing these stages during a crisis are described below.

I—Trust versus Mistrust

According to Erikson, trust versus mistrust is formed in the context of the infant's relationship with his mother: "But even under the most favorable circumstances, this stage seems to introduce into psychic life (and become prototypical for) a sense of inner division and universal nostalgia for a paradise forfeited. It is against this powerful combination of a sense of having been deprived, or having been divided, and of having been abandoned, that basic trust must maintain itself throughout life."[2]

This first stage of development is characterized by a nuclear conflict between trust and mistrust. It originally occurs between birth and twelve months of life but, as mentioned earlier, individuals continue to work on this conflict throughout the life cycle. Let's be realistic—no babies are probably ever so completely indulged that they completely overcome their initial "mistrustfulness." After all, the world in which they are to participate presents some very real dangers and pitfalls. Consequently, a certain residue of mistrust is no doubt essential.

However, to launch the child's ego properly in the difficult process of constructing an identity, it is desirable to have the balance tilt in the direction of trust.

A crisis reactivates unresolved feelings about basic trust because of the destruction of the belief that someone or something would always be there to support us. We all have a primitive fear of abandonment, and a crisis makes us feel as though we have been abandoned by everyone, including God. A crisis forces us to deal with our own essential "aloneness." Such an experience shakes the foundation of the personality. The feelings must be resolved before a new equilibrium and firmer integration can be attained.

When we are forced to recognize just how alone in the world we really are, we come to terms with some essential philosophical truths. The only unconditional commitment one can make is to oneself. That is the meaning of being a dying, alone, and independent individual identity. All other commitments are conditional. There are no guarantees. To deny this fact is to be deluded about the reality of human aloneness. Total interpenetrating oneness is one of the ideals of romantic love. We all want to believe that there will always be someone to comfort and nurture us—that mother's breast will never disappear. A crisis forces us to acknowledge that one can never depend totally on another person—a great deal, yes; but totally, no.

Among other things, loss teaches that there are no guarantees. It teaches that periodically we will be required to let go. It reminds us that we increase our vulnerability if we do not accept this fact.

But letting go and really feeling the loss that a crisis entails is a very difficult thing to do. It reminds me of an old Zen story.

... a student was searching for a teacher to show him the best way to live. After many weeks of traveling on the high mountain, he came to an Old Zen master's hut. It was a simple hut, sparsely furnished and absolutely clean. The old teacher invited him in and asked him to have a cup of tea. The student waited patiently as the water boiled for the tea. Finally, when it was ready, the teacher prepared a fine cup of tea. The student held out his cup to receive it, and the teacher poured the tea. He continued to pour and pour even after the cup was full. Soon the hot tea spilled out over the edges, burning the student's hand. The student cried out in alarm. "Why are you pouring hot tea over the edges like that?"

"Just like this cup," the teacher replied, "you are filled to the brim with yourself, your thoughts, feelings, and opinions. If you want to learn something from me, first you must empty your cup. You must make room for something new to enter."

Just like the teacher in the little hut, a crisis comes to help us to empty ourselves. It is trying to stir our awareness and to push us a little out of the lethargy we are experiencing. We are simply being taught to loosen our grip.

If we permit ourselves to fall into that abyss of anxiety and experience that pit of aloneness, we will discover that we can take it. We can experience our own ground. We can choose to validate ourselves and choose to make a commitment to ourselves. What we are essentially learning to do is to trust ourselves.

Erik Erikson believed that one of the key determinants of happiness is whether or not we will trust life. We have the choice of either saying "yes" or "no" to life. When you say "yes" your perceptions begin to change. That which seems so senseless no longer seems quite so terrible. Soon an inner power is felt. A belief begins to emerge that, no matter what the odds, it is possible to move forward in life.[3]

Just what does it mean to "trust life"? It does not mean trusting that life will always be good or that it will be free of grief and pain. It means trusting that somewhere inside yourself you can find the strength to go forth and meet whatever comes even if you meet betrayal and disappointment along the way. It means learning to live in the present, taking one day at a time. It also means pushing aside doubts that you can ever be happy again.

If we are truly to trust life we are going to need to learn to rely on friends and ask them for comfort. We are going to need to learn to share our feelings of loneliness, fear and hope with others. To trust life means to affirm that you are a good person. No one has to be perfect. That is an impossibility. It means to continue to go on trying.

Gail Sheehy believes that even when we know rationally that the alternative to change is stagnation, most of us fight it. This is due to the fact that we are extremely creative at finding ways to avoid risking change. We say *no* to life because we are afraid. Some of us must render the devil we know considerably worse than the devil we don't know in order to present ourselves with the rationale for taking a risk and making a change.[4]

Some of us are just simply afraid of making mistakes. I constantly remind myself and the people I work with that there is nothing wrong with making mistakes. As a matter of fact, *if you aren't making mistakes, its a bad sign.* You are probably not growing. In order to grow you must take risks. And a certain number of risks are bound to fail. But that's O.K. if we learn from our mistakes. I like to think that all of my mistakes are original ones. In other words, I don't make the some mistake twice—I try to learn from the first one and make the necessary inner or outer changes so that I don't repeat it. This is healthy, but the majority of people haven't learned to view failures, setbacks or mistakes in this same light.

Learning how to trust ourselves and to trust life is a lifetime process. This is a situation that is confronted at birth and is confronted again and again until the day we die. Each crisis gives us the opportunity to work on this important developmental issue.

Questions To Ask Ourselves:

1. Do I have unrealistic expectations about life?
2. Do I expect other people to meet needs of mine that I should be responsible for meeting myself?
3. Do I learn from my mistakes or do I constantly blame other people for my plight?
4. When a crisis hits, do I take the opportunity to reexamine my assumptions about the way things "ought to be" and learn how to better deal with how things really are?
5. Am I willing to go through the process of changing myself instead of trying to change the world?

Reflect: Behold, God is my salvation;
          I will trust and will not be afraid (Is 12:2).

Autonomy versus Shame and Doubt

Autonomy develops as children are given choices that they can freely make. This stage initially occurs from one year to three years. When a child is blocked in making such choices, the result is shame or doubt. "This stage . . . becomes decisive for the ration of love and hate, cooperation and willfulness, freedom of self-expression and its suppression. From a sense of self-control without loss of self-esteem comes a lasting sense of good will and pride; from a sense of loss of self-control and of foreign over-control comes a lasting propensity for shame and doubt."[5]

Erikson speaks of the nuclear conflict of the second stage of development as a struggle between a sense of "autonomy" on the one hand and a sense of "shame and doubt" on the other. Although the healthy child requires more of the former than of the latter, it is still necessary to strike a balance.

Erikson traces the origin of "will" or "willpower" in adulthood to this stage. This stage becomes decisive for the ration between loving good will and hateful self-insistence, between cooperation and willfulness, and between self-expression and compulsive self-restraint.

A crisis reopens this nuclear conflict of autonomy vs. shame and doubt. Persons who choose to live in a close relationship such as marriage give up a certain amount of their autonomy. Women especially may move from dependence upon parents to dependence upon a spouse without experiencing a time of being single and truly testing their autonomy.

As with the developing child, autonomous feelings are necessary for an adult to build an identity that is separate from parents, spouse, religion, society. The experience of a crisis may force us to learn behaviors that were previously taken care of by someone else.

I really had to do a lot of personal work around the issue of autonomy. I had assumed that my husband would always be there. It never even occurred to me how many things he had done for me until those things were no longer being done. I then had to learn to do them for myself.

Many widows reported the same experience when their husbands died. Some had never balanced a checkbook or handled any financial concerns. Others knew nothing about car repairs. Widowers and divorced men found they had to learn about household chores such as cooking and cleaning and childrearing when they were left alone.

Whenever we experience a crisis such as an illness, failure, rejection or loss, depression, a challenging task or an insurmountable obstacle, we are forced to face the fact that we are not very autonomous. These crises summon us to transcend our capabilities, our expectations, even our peace of mind. They interrupt or redirect the momentum of the autonomous self. They are points in life when the self must either expand or contract. Consciousness cannot remain neutral. Decisions must be made and consequences accepted. We are never the same afterward.

The opposite pole of autonomy is shame and doubt. After a crisis, the individual often feels ashamed at having failed in some way or another. We often feel that if only we had done something different, such a thing would never have happened to us. We can become doubtful about our ability to make good choices and exercise adequate control. We must therefore rework and solve the problems of shame and doubt, gain confidence in our own judgment, restore respect for self, and not be ashamed even if the world views the crisis as somehow our fault.

It is back to viewing mistakes or failures as opportunities to learn. I like to remind myself that a mistake at least proves somebody stopped talking long enough to do something. Few of us recognize the benefits of a mistake, failure or loss. We try instead to shield ourselves from it. Some people are strengthened by failure, and others are defeated by it. It has nothing to do with money or having more opportunities but depends more on personal character. You must be tough enough that you do not allow what happens in life to destroy you. The ability to survive is something very precious. The process of discovering that you have more courage than you ever thought possible is one of the precious rewards of facing and surviving a crisis.

Questions To Ask Ourselves:

1. How autonomous am I?
2. Have I neglected to learn tasks that every adult should know?
3. Am I using this crisis as an opportunity to learn new things about myself and the world in general?
4. Am I spending too much time berating myself for my past failures instead of learning from my mistakes and moving on?

Reflect: The kingdom of heaven is like a grain of mustard seed which a man took and sowed in his field; it is the smallest of all seeds, but when it has grown it is the greatest of shrubs and becomes a tree, so that the birds of the air come and make nests in its branches (Mt 13:31–32).

III—Initiative versus Guilt

The stage of initiative has much to do with the child becoming more sociable. It initially occurs between the ages of three and six years. Initiative is primarily concerned with exploration and creativity. The child in this stage is actively exploring all parts of the environment, testing powers to run and climb, take things apart and put them together, draw and paint.

Erikson believes that a general "ethos of action" can be traced to this third normative crisis. In other words, the problem of how to channel human energies may originate in childhood, but it remains an issue for adults as well. Children must begin to feel, and adults must retain the feeling, that their actions serve some purpose.

The crisis can now provide us with an opportunity to discover unexplored and undeveloped parts of our self. Time that was spent doing other things may now be used to discover new activities and learn new things about life. We need to take this time to reach out to the world. The following words put it very well:

> We all carry the cross-hatching of a thousand wounds. The wounds of childhood, still bleeding like the signs of the stigmata. The wounds of adolescence, still stinging with remembered pain. The bitter wounds of adult failures, or soured loves and lost dreams.
>
> How to make them all go away? How to become brave and young again? How to wipe the slate clean and re-enter the world like a tabula rasa, trusting and trustworthy again. I wish I knew.
>
> I only know the answer doesn't lie in learning how to protect yourself from life. It lies in learning how to strengthen yourself so you can let a bit more of it in.[6]

Those are very wise words but hard to remember when in the throes of a crisis. But they are imperative if we are to survive such an experience and grow. I know how hard it was for me to start over. Many mornings I dreaded getting out of bed. I just wanted to pull the covers up over my head and hide. I was so frightened.

In order to develop some initiative I had to start very slowly because I was so scared. I knew practically nothing about how to survive in the world. This is something I had relied on my husband to do for me. My fear was so great that I was unable to attempt anything new. I finally got to the place where I would give myself a little lecture. I'd say, "Well, Anita, you are a little late and slightly breathless, but better late than never!"

People who know me as I am today and patients with whom I share this experience find it very hard to believe that I was ever so immobilized by fear that I couldn't get out of bed. People see me as such a strong person. But it took much training to get me to this place. I literally had to force myself to do something, anything, as long as it got me out of the house. I would visit a friend, or hear a lecture, or do some volunteer work. This resulted in my nearly always feeling better afterward. So the next time I found myself unable to get out of bed in the morning, I would remember how good it felt that last time I forced myself into action. I would zero in on the good feelings that resulted and use those feelings to catapult me out of bed again. Each time it became just a little bit easier. The day finally came when I actually looked forward to getting up and going out into the world. I had finally developed age-appropriate initiative.

Guilt can result from poor handling of initiative and exploration, by violating one's values too much. We may be burdened with guilt over the crisis. Borrowing from the work of Dr. Peter Koestenbaum, guilt can be either neurotic or existential. Neurotic guilt stems from the superego. It results from early training. It is the experience of violating a rule that has been accepted irrationally or pre-rationally.

Existential guilt is much more valid. It comes from the fact that we are guilty of not fulfilling our potential. We therefore are angry at self-betrayal and furious at ourselves for our impotence. We become angry at ourselves, for we know that we are guilty of not taking charge of our lives. It is we who are guilty of neglecting our potential. It is the experience of existential guilt that can propel us into making much needed changes in our lives. We are always guilty of not fulfilling our potential. We always could be more than in fact we are.[7] This was certainly true in my own case.

The problem with developing initiative is that it involves risk and we are all very afraid to risk. The ultimate risk for anyone wanting to make a major change or attempt something new is that we are afraid that we will die from it. We forget that there are living deaths too. My refusal to get out of bed is a good example of this. "Obviously, to face reality can be frightening. It makes the necessity for change more real. And change involves the deepest sort of self-doubt. While struggling through change, you find yourself between two shells: your former identity is at least partially cracked, and a raw and fragile new identity is trying to form in the chilly air of uncertainty."[8] A part of us is dying and a new facet of our identity is being born. That is why a major change feels like a kind of death. *A part of us is dying.*

It is my belief that a major goal of personality development is to become self-actualized. According to Abraham Maslow, self-actualization is defined as an ongoing process of growth toward utilizing our potential. It takes initiative in order to do this. "Potential" is one's ultimate capacity for creative expression, interpersonal effectiveness, and fulfillment in living. If we are not actualizing our potential we will experience existential guilt. Any crisis affords us the opportunity to examine our conscience regarding this important developmental task.

Questions To Ask Ourselves:

1. How would I assess my level of initiative?
2. Do I allow fear to immobilize me?

3. Do I force myself to try new things because I know that it is important for my growth?
4. Do I suffer from neurotic guilt?
5. Do I suffer from the more important type of guilt—existential guilt?
6. What am I doing today to help me actualize more of my potential?

Reflect: I know how to be abased, and I know how to abound; in any and all circumstances I have learned the secret of facing plenty and hunger, abundance and want. I can do all things in him who strengthens me (Phil 4:12–13).

IV—Industry versus Inferiority

The school-age child begins to be a "worker and potential provider." At this stage the danger to children is that they may develop feelings of inadequacy and inferiority, if they compare themselves to others. Feelings of inferiority result from one's work being judged as poor or not worthwhile.

Erikson's "fourth age of man" encompasses the elementary school years. The channeling and direction of the child's energies that began during the previous stage must continue. Upon entering the school years the child begins to acquire the skills needed to work within the particular society. Learning these skills requires a certain degree of discipline. The more fortunate children emerge from the fourth stage of life with their self-esteem intact and a sense of industry that can later be translated into a sense of competence.[9]

After a crisis we may devalue aspects of our lives. We may feel totally incapable of doing anything different. We now may need to develop new competencies. Working through the nuclear conflict of industry vs. inferiority is again necessary if the future is to be worthwhile.

By reexperiencing this conflict, we will be forced to come face to face with the existential truth that as humans we are free but also responsible. We are in charge of our lives. Most of us are not willing to allow ourselves to experience the anxiety of what it means to risk making an authentic, existential decision. We continue to choose to avoid choosing, choose to resist owning our freedom by searching for answers or solutions. Experiencing a crisis may now force us to make changes. We are forced to be the agents of our actions, to be self-determined. A crisis forces us to take personal responsibility for our lives.

Again, a major reason that we are afraid to be industrious—to make necessary changes in our lives—is that we fear failure. We feel that we will not live up to our own idealized image of ourselves. According to Gail Sheehy, everyone in childhood conjures up an image of the idealized self—the person one would like to be. That ideal usually casts our virtues and desires in a mold so pure and nearly perfect that nothing could protect and preserve it. The dream of adolescence is always a little beyond our power to realize.[10]

The earlier that idealized image is cracked and we discover that we do not die from it, the sooner we can allow more self-compassion and humor inside and begin to accept that our identity will build, show blemishes, suffer injuries, repair itself and be renewed again and again, if we will just let it. *Therefore,* the best thing that can happen to us may be to fail a little early.[11]

We must learn how to overcome fear if we want to be more industrious just as we needed to do so in order to develop more initiative. The Buddha himself teaches us a valuable lesson on fear.

There is a Buddhist fable written over two thousand years ago about a beautiful young elephant who lived in the forest. She was as white as crane's down, according to the legend, and her size and strength were so great that the men who captured her gave her as a present to the king.

The king entrusted her to his elephant trainers to be taught to stand firm and to follow commands, but the trainers were harsh with her and beat her with their elephant goads, and one day, maddened by pain, she broke free of them and escaped.

She ran as fast as she could for many days, traveling as far into the Himalayan mountains as she could go, until she outdistanced all the king's men who were chasing her, and in time they all went home and she was free. But she still raced on, and although time passed she did not reduce her pace or forget for a moment that she had been a captive once. Every time a twig snapped or a breath of wind rustled the trees she dashed off at full speed, thrashing her trunk wildly from side to side.

Finally a compassionate tree sprite could stand her pain no longer and leaned out of a fork in a tree one day and whispered into the elephant's ear. "Do you fear the wind? It only moves the clouds and dries the dew. You ought to look into your mind. It's fear that has captured you." And the minute the wood sprite had spoken the beautiful elephant realized that she had nothing to fear but the habit of being afraid, and she began to enjoy life again.[12]

It is so easy to get into the habit of being afraid, but it is a very hard one to break. Many of us live most of our lives running and are constantly looking over our shoulders to see who or what is chasing us. Perhaps in the beginning someone was chasing us (such as an unhappy parent, an angry brother or some other perceived enemy). But we continue the habit of running long after the feared person is gone. If we are fortunate, some kind person like the tree sprite in our story will tell us to look again over our shoulder. And to our amazement, there is no longer anyone chasing us. We had simply forgotten to look.

I know that I spent many needless years running scared. I kept looking for someone to protect me from the world when what I needed to do was to learn how to trust myself. Each crisis I underwent only made me stronger. I began slowly but surely to develop my capacity to be industrious, and I learned in the process the wisdom of the words "If you don't decide which way to play with life, it always plays with you."[13]

Every crisis offers us another opportunity to work on the developmental issue of industry vs. inferiority. If we allow the crisis to give us an inferiority complex we are defeating its purpose. If we start saying to ourselves "How can this possibly have happened to me?" distress and anguish are sure to follow. But if your question is "What lesson can I learn from this?" growth and renewal will follow. Yesterday's disaster is today's teacher if we allow ourselves to linger past the pain to learn the lesson.

Questions To Ask Ourselves:

1. Am I taking the time to learn new skills and competencies in order to better prepare myself for the next stage of life?
2. Do I take personal responsibility for the course my life has taken?
3. Do I fear failure and allow this fear to immobilize me?
4. Have I allowed perfectionist tendencies to have an adverse impact on my self-esteem?
5. What am I doing today to help me learn how to conquer fear?

Reflect: Having gifts that differ according to the grace given to us, let us use them ... he who exhorts, in his exhortation; he who contributes, in liberality; he who gives aid, with zeal; he who does acts of mercy, with cheerfulness (Rom 12:6–8).

V—Identity versus Role Diffusion

Identity formation involves the discovery of who one is. Up to this point, as children continue to mature and assimilate the customs and values of their culture, they have inevitably learned a good deal about themselves. Their interactions with other people have begun to give them an impression of the characteristics they share with others and also of those that are unique to them alone. They have begun, in short, to formulate an identity. This process is, however, exceedingly complex, involving the ego in a continuous series of back and forth maneuvers.[14]

In order for an individual to formulate an identity, one must be able to entertain a number of different alternatives in quick succession. One's existence must be placed within what Erikson has termed an "historical perspective," evaluating the sort of person one has been in the past, the sort of individual one is at present, and the sort one has some chance of becoming in the future.

Aspects of our identity may need to be reworked as the result of a crisis. Any major life change forces us to look at ourselves and our situation anew. We may need to make changes in our lives as a result, and every change brings about the potential for loss. Sometimes a part of us must die so something new can be born. It is often hard to accept the fact that loss is a part of life.

Loss is like going through the birth canal. You are squeezed, pushed, disoriented, thrust from the known. This is the experience that a major crisis yields. Oftentimes our personal identity has not been allowed to formulate but rather is a superficial identity acquired to satisfy the expectations of society. A crisis or a loss can be a rebirth. We can make changes that are a better reflection of who we truly are.

The development of identity is appropriate for the adolescent stage of development. But especially in the case of women, a personal identity is discouraged during adolescence. Women of my generation were socialized to believe that the development of an authentic, independent identity was not important. Therefore, the resolution of this crisis of identity versus role confusion was not addressed. I certainly know that I had never resolved this issue and neither had the majority of the women that I had known. Successful resolution of this stage leads to a clear adult identity, while an unsuccessful resolution leads to a scattered, fragmentary, diffuse, shifting sense of who one is.

The development of the identity for females is further clouded by the so-called identity that society has given them. Women frequently move from the confines of the family to the structure of marriage without ever experiencing their own survival as an individual. The traditional role assigned to females is one of maternity and sexuality, or the role of another's identity. When the children leave, the woman is again "no one" and even the pretense of a real identity is lost.

Men, also, have problems with identity issues. The man who has not lived up to his own (and/or his wife's) expectations in his job or career is likely to have low self-esteem. Or the breadwinning man may be caught up in his work as his only source of feeling worthwhile. He may have been using work as a way to escape his family, or he may believe that he has to contribute to the welfare of his family by working. He may throw himself so fully into work that no time is allowed to develop other aspects of his personality.

Developing an independent individual identity is essential for psychological health. A person who has accomplished this has ego autonomy. The process of developing ego autonomy goes on throughout the individual's life cycle. It evolves. Ego autonomy is a concept that means a person is able to control his or her own life by adaptive choice and independent action. With ego autonomy, one has the inner freedom to develop one's potential both emotionally and intellectually. It implies the capacity to acknowledge reality in the process of making choices, but it does not mean "adjusting" to the status quo or to a specific social milieu. Ego autonomy calls for the ability to accept interdependence with other individuals, and in the process to benefit from these dependencies rather than be crippled by them.[15]

A crisis offers us an opportunity to again work on this crucial identity issue. Because our usual defenses are shaken, we experience the utter aloneness of being human. Out of this anguish we come face to face with our freedom and responsibility to actualize our potential. Our pain reminds us again of the fact that we are fully responsible for the creation of our own meaning. We will experience enormous existential guilt whenever we avoid developing ourselves into self-reliant and independent individual identities.

Questions To Ask Ourselves:

1. Do I know who I am?
2. Have I automatically adopted the values and attitudes of my parents, friends or spouse?
3. Do I know my values?
4. Am I capable of surviving in the world alone?
5. Am I willing to take a stand on important issues even if I know others will disapprove of me?
6. What am I doing today to work on my own personal identity?

Reflect:　But let each one test his own work, and then his reason to boast will be in himself alone and not in his neighbor. For each man will have to bear his own load (Gal 6:4–5).

VI—Intimacy versus Isolation

"The young adult ... is ready for intimacy ... the capacity to commit oneself to concrete affiliations and partnerships and to develop the ethical strength to abide by such commitments, even though they may call for significant sacrifices and compromises. ... The counterpart of intimacy is distantation: the readiness to isolate, and if necessary, to destroy those forces and people whose essence seems dangerous to one's own, and whose territory seems to encroach on the extent of one's intimate relations."[16]

In Erikson's view, a successful young adult must be able to express warmth and affection for others, and must be able to dis-

tinguish friends from enemies, but must also feel sufficiently secure to endure—and even to enjoy—being alone. The two major
preoccupations of adulthood, love and work, require a balance
between these two opposing trends. The individual who fears
closeness may withdraw from others and use work as a protective
shield. But the person who cannot bear to be alone, who can
never shut others out, cannot work.[17]

Experiencing a crisis gives us another opportunity to resolve
the conflict of intimacy vs. isolation. Naturally, isolation is probably felt by all persons who go through a crisis. We feel so alone.
No one could possibly understand what we are going through.
It is also a time when we desperately need others. Even if we have
never believed that close relationships were necessary, we find
ourselves in such pain that we are forced to reach out to others.
A crisis may enable us, for the first time in our lives, to see the
value of human connections. There is a wonderful old rabbinic
tale that illustrates this so well.

> The Lord said to the rabbi one day, "Come, I will
> show you hell." They entered a room where a group of peo-
> ple sat around a huge pot of stew. Everyone was famished
> and desperate. Each held a spoon that reached the pot but
> had a handle so long it could not be used to reach their
> mouths. The suffering was terrible.
> "Come, now I will show you heaven," the Lord said
> after a while. They entered another room, identical to the
> first—the pot of stew, the group of people, the same long
> spoons. But there everyone was happy and nourished. "I
> don't understand," said the rabbi. "Why are they happy
> here when they were miserable in the other room, and
> everything was the same?" The Lord smiled. "Ah, but
> don't you see?" he said. "Here they have learned to feed
> each other."[18]

I love this story because it is a reminder of how much we
need each other. This is especially true in times of crises.

But we also must recognize that to be human is to be alone. We must all come to terms with the Attachment–Separation polarity. If we become too separate, our contact with the world is lost and our capacity for survival jeopardized. If we become too attached to the environment or to another person, we endanger our capacity for self-renewal, growth and creative effort.

What does it mean to be intimate with another? Highly valued experiences in genuine interpersonal intimacy include the following: complete trust; validation of one's real impact on the world; constant stimulation to move toward new experiences; the experience of being of weighty significance in the personal life and growth of others; periods of transcendence from concern with self through devoted caring for and facilitating the other's well-being; periods of emotional and physical warmth, and closeness associated with an emergent state of belonging; freedom from role-bound segmentation; vicarious fulfillment through co-enjoying the shared joys of others; deepening one's comprehension of human suffering through co-pathic "vibrating" with the shared suffering of others.[19]

Intimacy is not symbiotic dependency. Many people enter relationships seeking completion in some fashion. They want the other person to make up for some lack they feel in themselves. They demand from others what they have not learned to give themselves. As a consequence, they attach themselves to another in hopes of getting needs met that each individual must meet for himself or herself. For example, a man who feels unlovable requires frequent assurances of his lovableness from his wife, or a highly dependent woman requires that her husband always be strong and not reveal his tender side. Such relationships are based on incompleteness and inequality and are not psychologically healthy.

A crisis forces us to work through the developmental conflict of intimacy vs. isolation. A death or a loss of major proportions makes it clear to us that if we want intimacy the time is now. It makes it clear just how important intimacy is as a value.

We now have the increased motivation to pursue close relationships with others.

A death or a divorce forces us to see what aspects of our lives were being fulfilled by another. Were we asking our significant other to live out parts of our personalities or to fulfill needs that we should have learned to meet for ourselves? If this has occurred, we now have the opportunity and the responsibility to learn to be full, complete, whole individuals and to take personal, solitary responsibility for the direction of our life.

Perhaps the best description of how to bridge the attachment/separation polarity comes from Kahlil Gibran:

> Love one another, but make not a bond of love:
> Let it rather be a moving sea between the shores of your souls.
> Fill each other's cup but drink not from one cup.
> Give one another of your bread but eat not from the same loaf.
> Sing and dance together and be joyous, but let each one of you be alone,
> Even as the strings of a lute are alone though they quiver with the same music.
> Give your hearts, but not into each other's keeping.
> For only the hand of Life can contain your hearts.
> And stand together yet not too near together:
> For the pillars of the temple stand apart,
> And the oak tree and the cypress grow not in each other's shadow.[20]

Questions To Ask Ourselves:

1. Do I have an adequate understanding of what it means to be intimate with another?
2. Have I developed my own identity so that I am capable of intimacy and not just symbiotic dependency?
3. Do I have the courage to reach out to other people even though I have been hurt before?

4. Have I taken the opportunity to grieve over past hurts and disappointments so that I don't take this "unfinished business" into future relationships?

Reflect: Two are better than one, because they have a good reward for their toil. For if they fall, one will lift up his fellow; but woe to him who is alone when he falls and has not another to lift him up. Again, if two lie together, they are warm; but how can one be warm alone? And though a man might prevail against one who is alone, two will withstand him. A threefold cord is not quickly broken (Eccl 4:9–12).

VII—Generativity versus Stagnation

"Generativity . . . is primarily the concern in establishing and guiding the next generation, although there are individuals wno, through misfortune or because of special and genuine gifts in other directions, do not apply this drive to their offspring. And, indeed, the concept of generativity is meant to include such more popular synonyms as productivity and creativity. . . . "[21]

Although young adults are more actively engaged in the community than the adolescent, their participation is still somewhat limited. Newly capable of intimacy, recently initiated into the world of work, they have yet to make their contribution to society in a larger sense. Ideally, this contribution is made during the seventh "age of man." Erikson believes such a contribution *must* occur if the mature adult is to retain the sense of wholeness and purpose.

If there is meaning in our lives, life becomes worthwhile. Life must have meaning or meaningful work. A healthy life is one that pursues such a goal. According to Viktor Frankl, a person who regards his life as meaningless is not merely unhappy but hardly fit for life. This is not only a matter of success and happiness but also of survival.

It is important for our lives to be a statement of who we are. Such a statement is eternal. As Frankl so well states: "Everything is written into the eternal record—our whole life, all our creations and actions, encounters and experiences, all our loving and suffering. All this is contained, and remains, in the eternal record."[22] According to Frankl, life is a lifelong question and answer period. As to the answers, we can only answer to life by answering for our lives. Responding to life means being responsible for our lives. The eternal record cannot be lost but neither can it be corrected. That is a warning and a reminder.

To have a sense of our own generativity is to understand what it means to be immortal. "It is true that we can't take anything with us when we die; but that wholeness of our life, which we complete in the very moment of our death, lies outside the grave and outside the grave it remains—and it does so, not although, but because it has slipped into the past. Even what we have forgotten, what has escaped from our consciousness, is not erased from the world: it has become part of the past, and it remains part of the world."[23]

We have a profound obligation to make sure that our lives in some way have mattered. If we don't, we will experience what Peter Koestenbaum describes as "ontological guilt." Such guilt is about "being" itself. According to Koestenbaum, part of ontological guilt is to appreciate the miracle and mystery of the fact that we do exist. "Ontological guilt is the ultimate commitment to living authentically, to living responsibility from the inside out, to taking personal charge of living exactly in accordance with what in one's heart one knows to be the truth. Ontological guilt is also gratitude for being; it is to recognize that being is an act of ontological grace quite out of our own hands. . . . Ontological guilt is guilt about existence. That is the most important guilt of all, for our deepest potential is to be rather than not to be."[24]

A crisis reminds us that time is running out. If we have wasted our lives and not fulfilled our potential, there may be no tomorrow. I really believe that for most of us, it takes something monumental to shake us from our lethargy. We always think that there will be a tomorrow and we need not rush. Shattering experiences remind us that this is not true. It is urgent that we live life now!

A crisis reawakens our existential anxiety and reminds us that one of life's most profound pains is to experience regret over unfulfilled possibilities. "The missed destiny can be a talent undeveloped, a love-relationship not pursued, sensuality that is untapped and not expressed, or a mind that has not been stretched by education. Neglect, inexcusable and perpetrated on ourselves and by ourselves, is the nature of existential guilt."[25]

Questions To Ask Ourselves:

1. Can I truly say that my life has meaning?
2. If I were to die tomorrow, what do I want people to remember about me?
3. What accomplishments am I proud of?
4. What do I still wish to accomplish before I die?
5. What am I doing today to make the world a better place?

Reflect: You are the light of the world. A city set on a hill cannot be hidden. Nor do men light a lamp and put it under a bushel, but on a stand, and it gives light to all in the house. Let your light so shine before men, that they may see your good works and give glory to your Father who is in heaven (Mt 5:14–16).

VIII—Ego Integrity versus Despair

Ego integrity is "the acceptance of one's one and only life cycle as something that had to be and that, by necessity, permitted of no new substitutions. . . . Despair expresses the feeling that the time is now short, too short for the attempt to start another life and try out alternate roads to integrity."[26]

In our culture and in many others, this final reckoning often brings images of despair to mind. Old people are thought to have lost their health and faculties. They are portrayed as becoming too weak, too disorganized, or too "set in their ways" for productive work, too much a relic of a generation past. No doubt people who must suffer through their last years in such a state are left to wonder if their lives did indeed have much validity.

However, as Erikson reminds us, there is another side to the nuclear conflict of old age and an alternative to despair. If elderly people can believe that they have met the crises of the previous stages with good grace and reasonable success, if they can believe that theirs has been a unique and worthwhile destiny, then a sense of integrity may predominate. Their ego and their identities have come through the life cycle intact, and their own lives can be placed at long last in a truly historical perspective.

Old age provides the final measure of identity. Near the end of their lives, individuals can determine how successful they were in coordinating their unique talents with their opportunities. Erikson designates wisdom as the enduring human virtue of this final epoch in the life cycle.[27]

This is the stage in life when we must answer the big questions: What have I done with my life? Did I use my God-given talents? Did I actualize my potential? What kind of statement have I made with my life? What will be the epitaph on my tombstone? We ask ourselves such questions in the winter of our lives. But knowing that we must answer such questions in our later years gives us the incentive to live life fully now.

Rabbi Kushner describes a person of integrity. Such a person is a "mensch." To be a mensch is to be the kind of person God had in mind when he arranged for human beings to evolve. A mensch is someone who is honest, reliable, wise enough to be no longer naive but not yet cynical, a person you can trust to give you advice for your benefit rather than his or her own. Such a person acts not out of fear or out of the desire to make a good impression but out of a strong inner conviction of who he or she is and what he or she stands for. A mensch is not a saint or a perfect person but a person from whom all falsehood, all selfishness, all vindictiveness have been burned away so that only a pure self remains.[28]

To be a person of integrity, as Kushner so aptly describes, should be the goal of all of our lives. But so many of us look for happiness in the wrong places, such as in pleasureable experiences. It never occurs to us that happiness is not the true goal in life. The true goal is a task that continues right up to the end, namely, the most complete and comprehensive development of the personality. It is this which gives life an incomparable value that can never be lost. If we have achieved wholeness by developing all aspects of our personality, we will experience a sense of inner peace as a result. And with this peace, we will experience the highest form of happiness that life has to offer.

As Schopenhauer says: "The first forty years of life furnish the text, while the remaining thirty supply the commentary; without the commentary we are unable to understand aright the true sense and coherence of the text, together with the moral it contains."[29]

To refuse to grow and develop our potential is what I define as "sin." Kierkegaard equates sin with the despair of "not willing to be oneself," a flight response of the individual to the dread of autonomy. If it turned out that hell were nothing more than the experience of coming face to face with our empty life, a life completely devoid of meaning, such pain would be enough. I would imagine that the pain of looking back over one's life with a sense of existential disgust would be unbearable. God did not have to create hell as our punishment because we will have created it for ourselves.

Growing old is the inescapable lot of all of God's creatures. But growing old meaningfully is a task ordained for humanity alone. What meaning has our life? It has none but that which we give it. This is what integrity is all about. We either come to the end of our life with a sense of integrity or are doomed to unadulterated despair. The choice is ultimately ours. A crisis can be a vivid reminder of this unalterable fact.

Questions To Ask Ourselves:

1. Am I living my life as fully and authentically as possible?
2. Am I working every day at achieving my potential?
3. Am I using my God-given talents?
4. Am I being true to myself by being honest in my dealings with myself as well as with other people?
5. What am I doing today to insure that my life has integrity?

Reflect: He who walks blamelessly, and does what is right,
and speaks truth from his heart;
who does not slander with his tongue,
and does no evil to his friend,
nor takes up a reproach against his neighbor;
in whose eyes a reprobate is despised,
but who honors those who fear the Lord;
who swears to his own hurt and does not change;
who does not put out his money at interest,
and does not take a bribe against the innocent.
He who does these things shall never be moved
(Ps 15:2–5).

Utilizing Erikson's Theory for Growth

As you can see, Erikson's theory of psychosocial development can help you during a crisis. Depending on your age, the appropriate developmental issues will be reactivated. You are being given another opportunity to resolve these nuclear crises. If you take this opportunity that life is currently providing, you will not have to fear arriving at the winter of your life in a state of despair. You will have become a person of integrity. It is never too late to work on these issues. A crisis is survivable and provides us with a tremendous challenge.

Robert Veninga, in *A Gift of Hope*, discusses how people survive their tragedies. He believes that those people who are fortunate to have survived a heartbreak have engaged in what Dag Hammarskjold once referred to as "the longest journey, the journey inward." The difficulties of this pilgrimage are aptly stated by Carl Jung: "Whenever there is a reaching down into innermost experience, into the nucleus of personality, most people are overcome by fright, and many run away.... The risk of inner experience, the adventure of the spirit, is alien to most human beings."[30]

Once again, it is those painful times in our lives that afford us the opportunity to work on all of these developmental issues. None of these issues are resolved once and for all. There are going to be periods in our lives when we will need to work through them again. We really should be working on them all the time, not just when a crisis hits. But because we are human, we successfully ignore them when times are good. It usually takes a major crisis to remind us that these issues are still there.

A crisis of sufficient proportions reactivates all of Erikson's nuclear conflicts that a person has formerly resolved. A crisis is also a foreshadower of conflicts that have not yet been resolved or perhaps even addressed. The opportunity to develop and grow from these experiences awaits us all.

Chapter 3

—————— • ——————

Crisis: What It Means
To Be Human

I was very fortunate during a difficult time in my life to come across the work of Dr. Peter Koestenbaum. He is a well known philosopher and author whose ideas and theoretical concepts made a great deal of sense to me. He was both a teacher and a mentor and had a significant impact on my life. He helped me become aware of how I could learn to view my pain in a positive manner by suggesting that my pain was my personal reminder of what it means to be truly human. I could use my pain to teach me about life.

Dr. Koestenbaum also taught me how I could use philosophy as a coping device. Philosophy could help me adjust to life, make sense of my suffering, and find meaning in my symptoms. It could help me to acknowledge, tolerate, and then overcome and transcend the evils and the injustices that I was experiencing.

His theories helped me tremendously during times of major crises. They made a great deal of sense and helped me make a friend of pain. Seeing pain in a positive light was very important because, as I mentioned earlier, I was so frightened of it as a child. I spent many years running away from pain because I did not have faith that I could confront it and survive. I had not yet allowed myself to be "schooled in pain."

Before I came into contact with Dr. Koestenbaum, I had a very naive attitude about life and what it means to be human. I had never studied philosophy and I was not familiar with the works of the great philosophers such as Kierkegaard, Heidegger,

Nietzsche, etc. If I had been, I could have learned some very important truths about the human condition. I would have been aware of the impact that the discipline of philosophy has had on contemporary problems. The wisdom of the ages is contained in philosophical writings which could have taught me a great deal about life.

If I had been a student of philosophy, I would have begun to see the value of pain at an earlier age and would have realized the important part pain plays in human growth. Learning these truths has greatly helped me understand that my suffering and struggles were not due to my being a bad person. I had previously equated pain with punishment. It never occurred to me that pain was simply a part of life and a necessary prerequisite for growth.

After many years as a philosopher, Dr. Koestenbaum developed a new discipline which combined the best of philosophy with the best of therapy and called it "clinical philosophy." I was fortunate to receive significant training in this new field. I would like to share with you some of the principles of clinical philosophy because I believe that it is another way of viewing a crisis.

We can use the experience of a crisis in order to rework developmental issues as discussed in depth in Chapter 2. But in addition to offering us that invaluable opportunity, a crisis can also teach us just what it means to be human. Philosophy can help us put our pain in a context where we can begin to view it in a much more productive way.

What Is Clinical Philosophy?

Clinical philosophy is the disciplined use, in the service of the healing arts, of those insights about persons that traditionally have been the province of philosophy and the humanities. It is the belief that a workable philosophy of life ranks next in importance to the survival basics of food, shelter, and clothing. Beyond that, clinical philosophy seeks to isolate and heal the universal, inescapable, and profound human paradoxes that are a part of life. These underlying philosophic themes cut to the heart of human existence, painfully exposing the ultimate truth of our destiny as human beings. Philosophy may be the only vehicle to understanding major crises.[1]

Clinical philosophy systematically explores and applies one idea: human problems are tied to what we call the philosophic truths about human existence. Clinical philosophy answers these questions: What are the basic tenets that describe human beings? What are the basic tenets that describe the world in which we live?[2]

Health is meaningful only to the extent that we express in life these basic principles. Philosophic insight into the eternal questions of human existence is a prerequisite for the experience of meaning, success, fulfillment, joy, peace, authenticity and health.

A well-trained clinical philosopher possesses a comprehensive and a clear idea of what it means to be human and to be a person and uses that information as a tool to search out the central issues in life and thereby learns how to be authentic. Each of us needs to learn how to be a clinical philosopher. This can greatly help us when times are difficult and we begin to ask the kinds of questions that appear to have no answers.

One of the principles of clinical philosophy is that each person needs a philosophy of life, which includes a philosophic grasp of human reality. Human problems are really the result of philosophic ignorance. Unless we learn the truths of human reality we can neither understand nor resolve human problems.[3]

The type of human problems that concern clinical philosophy are dilemmas that for the most part do not have anything that traditionally would have a solution. A crisis oftentimes is one of these dilemmas with no solution. Death has no solution nor does the problem of aloneness. Losses which are of major proportions are universal experiences without any right answers. No one deserves to have such things happen. These are just aspects of the human condition that don't have solutions. We may demand that the crises of death, meaning, aloneness, loss be met. Emotionally we expect these problems to have answers but logically we know that they do not.[4] Any of us who have experienced a major crisis know this to be true.

The first level of wisdom in clinical philosophy is to realize that these dilemmas with no solution are at the heart of our problems. They demand answers but there are no answers. Unanswerable questions are not isolated or rare. They are the daily undercurrent of most of our experiences. Understanding the truth of this is extremely important. We are powerless vis-à-vis the great forces of the universe. That is a philosophic reality for all of us and it is an insoluble problem.[5]

According to clinical philosophy, the proper response to unanswerable problems is to both experience and explore them. Anytime people experience a major crisis such as the loss of a loved one or face a serious illness, they are really experiencing one of these types of problems. Some philosophic truth is revealed in whatever human problem they are suffering.

The Truths About Human Existence

Just what are these unadorned truths about human beings? Some examples are death, freedom, meaning, intimacy, aloneness, commitment, embodiment, trust, anxiety, guilt, and many more. For example, it is a person's essence to be, that is, to exist; it is a person's essence to be free, that is, to be a self-determiner. Philosophic truths are like grooves in our consciousness. They are the archetypes, those forces which organize our behavior, beliefs, and expectations. They are patterns of reality and factors in experience.[6]

These truths represent the universally true essence or nature of persons and they are independent of culture, sex, age and socio-economic status. They evolve and follow a developmental pattern that continues over a lifetime. At some point in our life we will be forced to concern ourselves with such mysteries as the power of human freedom, the finality of dark death, the dive into the pit of aloneness, the fall into the unending abyss of anxiety, the despair of guilt, the passion of commitment, the comfort of gentle love, the hope of coming home, finding ground or roots, and the eternal peace of consciousness as the silent and solitary center.[7]

Clinical philosophers view anxiety not as a disease but as a revelation and direct experience of the lack of ground that we all suffer in this world. Thus, anxiety puts us in touch with these truths about human existence and should therefore be viewed positively.

Access to these truths about life is the secret of authenticity, fulfillment and health. Health means to live in conformity with these principles. The greater our understanding of them and the more complete their integration into our life, the more authentic and healthy we will be. Our lives will be successful to the extent that these truths are integrated into our existence. To the degree that they are not integrated, our lives will not work.[8] This is precisely why it is so important that we have a good grasp of them. I can tell you from my own personal experience that a crisis will force us to come to terms with them. Thus, a crisis really becomes an opportunity to learn more about what it means to be human.

As I mentioned earlier, when we are experiencing a crisis we are really facing one of these philosophical truths. It is important to confront the deeper issue involved in any particular crisis. If a loved one dies or leaves, we must deal with our aloneness as well as confront the issue that all of us are dying beings. If we must make a major decision that has no right answer, we confront the issues of freedom, meaning, and individual identity.

There is really no way to avoid these essential truths. For as long we resist dealing with them, life will continue to confront us with them. Our lives will not work until we deal with them. Such philosophic self-disclosure and psychological maturation meets resistances, repression, denial, defenses and self-deception. The reasons are fear of pain, philosophic ignorance, and natural inertia. We simply refuse to face these issues and many of us will die continuing to resist this insight.

When we are experiencing a life crisis, we are already in tremendous pain. So why waste our sorrows. Our pain can teach us about life. It is an undeniable fact that life will eventually force us into a position of such intense pain that we will have no choice but to consider the truth of these philosophical truths about existence. Let's learn to use this pain to our advantage. It takes tremendous courage to do this but the result will be very beneficial.

When you allow yourself to confront one of these truths about human existence, you will find yourself experiencing what clinical philosophy calls an "existential crisis." Any major crisis that forces you to confront one of these essential truths can be termed an "existential crisis." For example, if a loved one has died, you are dealing with more than the loss of that person. You are also being exposed to some important philosophical realities. You are facing your essential aloneness. You are confronting the reality of death, your own as well as that of loved ones. When facing death, it reminds you of the fact that life is truly precious and the responsibility of living it fully must be acknowledged. If you were so closely attached to the loved one that you had neglected your own growth, you will have the opportunity to work on the philosophical fact that you are a separate individual.

The philosophical facts about a person's essential human nature can be taught at any time. It is the act of permitting the discovery within yourself of what you truly are. But human nature being what it is, it usually takes a crisis for most of us to face these facts. I remained ignorant of them until a crisis put me in such a state of anxiety and pain that I was forced to ask the bigger questions about life. Here is where clinical philosophy was so much help to me. It put me in touch with the fact that every normal and healthy person suffers from conditions that are essential to existence itself, and these conditions respond only to appropriate philosophical insight.

After having gone through an "existential crisis," I would

heartily agree with Koestenbaum that such an experience is perhaps the most painful, difficult, agonizing, profound, proud, noble and satisfying event in the life of any human being. The existential crisis involves the decision for redefinition and reperception of the self and the world. Anyone who is in a crisis can use this opportunity to make it an existential one by facing the relevant truths of human existence.

Another way of explaining the "existential crisis" is to describe it as the experience and exploration of a human problem in its fullest. It is a rebirth experience. The general rule is that the deeper and more painfully we allow ourselves to experience one of these philosophical truths, the greater sense of security will be attained. If we truly allow ourselves to feel how alone we are as human beings, to experience the pain of that truth to the depth of our being, the stronger our ego becomes as a result. We increase our freedom and control over life in direct proportion to the felt anxiety. This is what it means to own one's existence.[9]

After experiencing depression and then despair we can learn to cope with these philosophical truths. Health is defined by clinical philosophy as access to these truths of human existence, ownership of them and the integration of them in our life.

In order to avail ourselves of the opportunity to use the present crisis as a means of dealing with these important philosophical truths, let us discuss some of the major ones in depth. A complete and thorough description of these truths are contained in Peter Koestenbaum's books entitled *The Existential Crisis* and *The New Image of the Person*. A brief summary of the major truths of human existence along with relevant examples are listed below.

1. Death

The real issue in life is that it will end. We are all terminally ill. Death makes us see the seriousness of life and motivates us to take charge of it. How many more days do we have left before we die? Such confrontation with the ultimate reality of the inescapable truth of death can lead to supreme courage and seriousness about life.

Most of us have great difficulty taking our own lives seriously. We may invest ourselves in others' lives far more fully then we invest in our own. We must consistently challenge ourselves to take seriously the fact that we are dying, that life is limited, that the number of good years ahead may be less than we realize.

At the time of my divorce, I became painfully aware of how little energy I had spent in self-development. There were many talents that I was not using and that I was allowing to lie dormant. When I began to realize that I was a dying being, it became very important for me to begin to live my life more fully. A crisis is a vivid reminder that time is running out.

Few of us can bear the thought that we are doing everything else *but* attending to our own seriousness about life. It is our destiny to die. In clinical philosophy we confront the universal truth that every person is mortal every moment of his or her life. Our interest is to uncover the meaning of our finitude and our mortality.[10] If we allow ourselves to truly come to terms with the philosophical truth about death, we will begin to recognize the seriousness of life. A crisis is just another reminder of this reality.

Questions To Ask Ourselves:

1. How many good years do I realistically believe I have left before I die?
2. Upon my death, what do I want people to remember about me?
3. Do I have some unfinished business that I should take care of before I die?
4. Can I honestly say that I am living my life to the fullest now?
5. Am I taking my life seriously?

Reflect: I have fought the good fight, I have finished the race, I have kept the faith. Henceforth there is laid up for me the crown of righteousness, which the Lord, the righteous judge, will award me on that Day, and not only to me but also to all who have loved his appearing. (2 Tim 4:7–8)

2. Freedom and Responsibility

Another important truth of existence is that of freedom and responsibility. The two go hand in hand. It is important to own our responsibility for being in charge of our lives. Freedom is very easy to deny especially in view of deterministic and fatalistic views of human nature. Many of us have never made a real decision—an existential choice. Oftentimes, the search for the "right" or "correct" answer is a decision to avoid making a decision. That is why in clinical philosophy we talk about insoluble problems. A choice is real only when right answers do not exist or are irrelevant.

A crisis may force us into the position of having to make an existential choice. Most of us are not willing to allow ourselves to experience the anxiety of what it means to risk making an authentic, existential decision. We continue to avoid choosing, resist choosing and resist owning our freedom by searching for answers, solutions or "the truth."

Whenever people make decisions, they are producing something that did not exist before. It cannot be undone. It is final. That is the nature of a choice and a big reason why people resist them. We don't like the fact that we will then be responsible for our choices. We fail to realize that to choose to not make a decision is still a decision.

Sometimes we tell ourselves that we have been victimized by life and blame others for our problems. But to confront the issues of freedom and responsibility puts our life back into our own hands. Self-pity, paranoia, victimization, martyrdom, etc.

are the signs of not taking charge freely and voluntarily of one's
own life.

One of the signs that we have contacted this important truth
is the sense that we ourselves are the agents of our actions, that
we are self-determined. We are acting authentically whenever
we tolerate a difficult situation. We tolerate it not because we
must, or have to, or should or ought to, but because we want to,
plan to and choose to.

Whenever we refuse to do something effective about an unsatisfactory life situation, we are denying the truth of our freedom and responsibility. If we continue to confront ourselves with
our freedom, we will no longer feel self-pity or impotence. We
become aware of the fact that what we do is in fact done by us,
that we act always as we choose to act. It is no longer possible to
deny this fact.[11]

No matter whether we are facing a developmental crisis or
an unexpected, accidental crisis, we are being called upon to
make changes in our life. There is no getting around this fact.
We are free to do with our lives what we want but we are at the
same time responsible for the results. We do not have the power
to change fate but we certainly have the power to change ourselves.

Some say life is like a Greek tragedy, our doom apparent
to all from the first scene. The script is lying there on the
table for anyone astute enough to read. Some feel we have
work to do in this life left over from the one before. And
those whom the gods take kindly to, they give a lot of pain,
so that it will move them along faster to that place where
they're meant to be. And there are those who believe that
there are things that we must learn early on, which, if not
learned then, hold us up in the next stage. I only know that
we each are dealt a hand, and most of us seem to play it,
and few of us think to say, "I don't want these cards" or
"Could you deal again?"[12]

Questions To Ask Ourselves:

1. Do I accept responsibility for my life?
2. Do I really recognize that I am in charge of my life?
3. Do I have problems making decisions or setting goals?
4. Would other people describe me as a martyr or a victim?
5. Have I ever really made an existential choice—one that had no right answer?

Reflect: Rise up early in the morning and stand before Pharaoh, and say to him, "Thus says the Lord, the God of the Hebrews, 'Let my people go, that they may serve me' " (Ex 9:13).

3. Aloneness and Isolation

To be human is to be essentially alone. We come into this world alone and we die alone. To confront the truth of aloneness and isolation is to recognize that we all have been abandoned. To be human is to be isolated, lonely, finite, without help or support.

The need for love, companionship, commitment, community and God emanates from the experience of abject and painful aloneness. These values derive their urgency from the despair of aloneness. Love allows us to share our aloneness.

Many psychological problems are the result of not owning up to one's freedom and of denying the reality and inevitability of our aloneness. Every human being, regardless of appearances to the contrary, stands alone! This fact must be understood and confronted before an authentic life becomes a realistic possibility.

The human condition requires contact with the tragic sense of life. Anyone who has experienced a major crisis knows this is true. Knowing this fact is a source of profound wisdom. Perhaps nothing is more tragic in life than being completely alone. Each of us must search for ways to cope with this terrifying emptiness.

In an existential crisis, the individual who is experiencing aloneness has the opportunity to transform this from anxiety to security, from despair to joy. The source of many troubles in life lies in not fully allowing ourselves to experience what it means to stand alone. We lack adequate command over the essential human truth of isolation.

It is sad to see how many people will sacrifice their values, their roots, their meaning, their happiness, even their lives, in the hope of not being abandoned. This is because we are so afraid of facing the horror of total aloneness. People stay in bad relationships and unfulfilling jobs and sacrifice personal integrity to avoid any possibility of abandonment. This results in self-betrayal.

To the degree that one denies the reality of aloneness as central to one's existence, life will not work out. The only unconditional commitment in the world is to oneself. All other commitments are conditional. Only to the degree that one is emotionally prepared to give up a relationship is there a realistic chance for the relationship to work. To choose to give up a significant relationship is to risk aloneness. We have to believe that it is far better to be alone than to be in a bad relationship. If we believe that, we will then have the strength to demand a good relationship.

I cannot tell you how many times the issue of aloneness becomes relevant in therapy with patients. Everyone wants a good relationship with another person. But few are willing to pay the price that is required for a good relationship. The price is the ability to tolerate aloneness. If you can accept being alone, you will be unwilling to settle for an unsatisfactory relationship. You will not take abuse. When you get to the place where you are strong enough to stand alone, a healthy relationship becomes a real possibility.

A Hasidic story tells of a man who went for a walk in a forest and got lost. He wandered around for hours trying to find his way back to town, trying one path after another, but none of them led out. Then abruptly he came across another hiker walking through the forest. He cried out: "Thank God for another human being. Can you show me the way back to town?" The other man replied, "No, I'm lost too. But we can help each other in this way. We can tell each other which paths we have already tried and been disappointed in. That will help us find the one that leads out."[13]

This story reminds us that we can ask others for support, encouragement and advice, but no one can live our life for us. We each have the sacred responsibility to find our own way. Aloneness is natural. It is normal, it is right, and it is painful. In not facing this fact, we are resisting human reality. Aloneness is not a negotiable situation.[14]

Questions To Ask Ourselves:

1. Do I recognize the fact that I came into this world alone and that I will leave this world alone?
2. Do I cling to other people in order to avoid facing my aloneness?
3. Do I tolerate unacceptable behavior from others in order to insure that I will not be abandoned?
4. Am I able to take a stand on controversial issues?
5. Am I too dependent on others? Do I rely on others to meet needs that I alone am responsible for meeting?

Reflect: My God, my God, why hast thou forsaken me?
          Why art thou so far from helping me, from the words
              of my groaning?
          O my God, I cry by day, but thou dost not answer;
              and by night, but find no rest (Ps 22:1).

4. Meaning and Work
We derive our self-esteem and sense of worth from meaning and work. If there is meaning, life is worth living. A life that

does not feel itself successfully moving or striving toward some meaning develops symptoms. A healthy life is one that successfully pursues a meaning. We must ask ourselves the question: What is it that gives meaning to our life? Any person who is worrying about the meaning of life is proving his or her humanness. A life which feels fulfilled is in pursuit of meaning. The by-products of this search are pleasure, happiness, power and potency.[15]

Oftentimes, when a crisis hits, we lose the meaning from our lives as well. It can be very devastating when a dream dies. It is my belief that God never closes one door without opening another. We may find that we have to dream new dreams.

When my marriage ended and my family structure came apart, it felt as if all the meaning in my life had gone. It was on one of the darkest days of my life that I received a phone call expressing interest in my first manuscript. The phone call reminded me that all was not lost. I was more than a wife and a mother. There were many other possibilities for my future that I had never even envisioned.

It is very normal to want to isolate yourself at the time of a crisis, to lose hope in ever living a meaningful life again. But isolating yourself is one of the worst things you can do. I always tell people that they must walk out into the sunshine looking up if they are to see the new door opening. If you stay inside and close yourself off, you won't be able to avail yourself of the opportunity to create new meaning in your life. The repression of our will to meaning can cause us to feel that life has no purpose, no challenge, no obligations; that it makes no difference what we do; that life is overpowering; that we have no more significance than an insect under a steamroller. We feel hopelessly trapped by circumstances beyond our control. We are "stuck," defeated by life. Life is a rat race, a treadmill, and there is a vast emptiness in us. The existential vacuum exists among rich and poor, young and old, the successes and the failures.

People respond with relief when they are assured that their

feeling of inner emptiness is by no means a symptom of mental disease but rather a challenge to fill this emptiness. This is a challenge to which only a human being can rise. People can find strength in the message that their feeling of meaninglessness is not a symptom of sickness but proof of their humanness. Only humans can **feel** the lack of meaning because only they are aware of this fact. It is our sacred responsibility to create meaning in our lives. We each have to do this for ourselves.

> God gives the birds their food, but he does not throw it into their nests (Greek proverb).

Questions To Ask Ourselves:

1. Can I honestly say that my life has meaning?
2. Do I feel fulfilled?
3. Do I enjoy my work?
4. What are my values? Am I living my life in accordance with these values?
5. What can I do today to add meaning to my life?

Reflect: As each has received a gift, employ it for one another, as good stewards of God's varied grace (1 Pet 4:10).

5. Anxiety

Anxiety is another truth about reality. It is the experience of the lack of ground that all humans experience. We have all experienced separation anxiety—it is a universal human condition. We are experiencing in separation anxiety the anxiety of nihilism or of nothingness—the discovery that there is no foundation, no answer. It is the groundlessness of human existence and the realization that to be human is to be alone and abandoned.

To be human is to be anxious. Anxiety is the experience of deconstitution and death but is also a prerequisite for meaningful change and growth. Anxiety is a signal to us that change is needed. That is why every developmental transition involves tremendous anxiety. A midlife crisis is a good example of this. The reason we are anxious is because we need to make changes in our lives in order to grow and evolve. If there was no anxiety we would lack the motivation necessary to make the needed change. To deny anxiety is to deny our essential aliveness.

According to Koestenbaum, existential anxiety is the unique phenomenon of human experience that reveals our transcendental truth. It is healthy, normal and desirable and should be cultivated and is a condition that leads to strength and creativity. "Existential anxiety reveals the reality of consciousness, our nature as a field, the abyss and the search for ground residing in our depth, the vastness of our freedom, and all of those characteristics of our essence needed to achieve true health."[16]

When we deny anxiety, we deny our true nature. The health of a person can be measured by the extent of his or her toleration for anxiety. A healthy person has an enormous capacity for being comfortable with anxiety. Anxiety is tolerated when we abandon ourself to it and gain strength and stature from this experience. We achieve ego strength through the toleration of anxiety.

A positive way to view anxiety is that to be anxious is to be alive! The search for meaning is brought about through the phenomenon of anxiety. The emptiness of anxiety makes love and compassion all the more important. We see the importance of such values when we experience the anxiety of isolation, separation and abandonment.

The presence of anxiety is positive because it is a sign that something within us is about to be born. The old self is dying and a new self is trying to be born. We are growing, and, as I mentioned earlier, no growth will ever occur without anxiety. Therefore, anxiety should be viewed as a friend and not as an enemy.

Questions To Ask Ourselves:

1. How well do I respond to anxiety?
2. Do I allow myself to listen to the message my anxiety is trying to give me?
3. How much anxiety can I tolerate? Am I working on building up my anxiety tolerance?
4. What changes do I need to make in my life?
5. Is there a new part of me that is trying to be born?

Reflect: Do not be anxious about tomorrow, for tomorrow will be anxious for itself. Let the day's own trouble be sufficient for the day (Mt 6:34).

6. Individual Identity

This philosophical truth was discussed in Chapter 2 in conjunction with Erikson's fifth stage of man—Identity versus Identity Confusion. Individual identity involves the decision to be an individual and to become divorced from mom and dad. One's individual and unique identity is not a *fait accompli* but a personal responsibility that is freely and fully assumed. In so doing, we must risk saying "no" to traditional sources of support such as God, country, parents, society, etc. When we say "no" to such supports we say "yes" to our individuality. This causes much anxiety, alienation and loneliness but results in pride, nobility and strength.[17]

I was confronted with this truth when I was in my early thirties and realized I had no personal identity. I had previously defined myself by my relationships with my husband and children. If they were doing well, then I was doing well. I was the woman who had no name. I was Bill's wife, Steve, Scott and Chris' mother, Paul and Jeanne's daughter and Paula's sister. But I had no sense of an individual identity. My anxiety over this was tremendous, and it was this anxiety that spurred me on to write my first book *Seasons: Women's Search for Self Through Life's Stages*.

I had much work to do on developing my own individual identity. This is an especially important issue for women who have been socialized to achieve their identity through others. But men can also suffer from a lack of an individual identity if they have allowed themselves to be defined by the expectations of others.

All of us have to grow and learn to meet our own needs. We can't continue, like children, to expect our needs to be met by someone outside of ourselves. It is our responsibility to become self-determined individuals with resources of our own.

There is an ancient Iranian allegory written in the thirteenth century by Farid ud-din Attar about the Simurgh, an immortal bird who makes his nest in the branches at the top of the tree of knowledge. One day one of the Simurgh's silver feathers is found in the middle of China, and the other birds, tired of being without a leader, decide to seek him out so that he can give their lives some direction. They know only that his name means "thirty birds" and that he makes his castle in the Kaf, the range of mountains that rings the earth.

At the outset some of the birds lose heart and claim they cannot make the trip. The nightingale pleads his love for the rose, the parrot pleads his beauty for which he lives caged. The partridge cannot leave his home in the hills, the heron his home in the marshes, the owl his ruins. But finally a delegation of birds sets out on this perilous venture. They travel for many days and years and cross through seven valleys and seas, the last two bearing the names Bewilderment and Annihilation. Many of the pilgrims desert, and the journey takes its toll among the rest. Finally thirty birds made pure by their suffering reach the great peak of the Simurgh. At last they behold him, and they realize that they are the Simurgh, and that the Simurgh is each and all of them.[18]

Questions To Ask Ourselves:

1. How would I answer the question "Who am I?"
2. Have I neglected to develop my individual identity?
3. What am I currently doing to insure my own personal growth?
4. Am I able to make independent decisions?
5. What about myself can I truly say is unique or different?

Reflect: But we exhort you, brethren, to do so more and more, to aspire to live quietly, to mind your own affairs, and to work with your hands, as we charged you, so that you may command the respect of outsiders, and be dependent on nobody (1 Thes 4:10–12).

7. Guilt

This philosophical truth was discussed in Chapter 2. As you will recall, there are several kinds of guilt. Neurotic guilt is the introjection of external authority. Existential guilt is the knowledge that we deliberately deny needed growth. We have not lived up to our expectations or fulfilled our potential. We have betrayed ourselves. Such feelings of guilt lead to our taking responsibility for our lives and are therefore necessary for growth and change. We also are existentially guilty for not having adequate command over the other truths about human existence.

I see a great deal of existential guilt in my practice. I work in an affluent community which houses many extremely successful, middle aged professionals. They come to therapy with all the symptoms of "meaninglessness" asking themselves "Is this all there is?" They work very hard, put in long hours, and have all the material possessions that money can buy. But they are depressed and anxious. They report that they feel like frauds and cannot understand why.

What has happened is that their values have no substance. They are unfulfilled and living meaningless lives. It is no wonder that they are experiencing existential guilt. The experience of guilt can be very positive if the individual makes needed changes in life as a result. It is signaling the need to reappraise one's life and set new directions. It could be a change in values, a new career, the development of unacknowledged parts of the personality, etc. If one's life is to be fulfilling and meaningful, existential guilt must be addressed. A crisis is an opportunity to work on these issues.

Questions To Ask Ourselves:

1. Am I fulfilling my potential?
2. Do I use my God-given talents to the best of my ability?
3. Can I honestly say that I am happy with my life?
4. What changes do I need to make in my life to reduce my existential guilt?

Reflect: There is an evil I have observed under the sun, and a grave one it is for man, that God sometimes grants a man riches, prosperity and wealth, so that he does not want for anything, but God does not permit him to enjoy it. If a man begets a hundred children and lives many years, but never finds contentment, I would say that a stillborn child not even accorded a burial is more fortunate than he (Eccl 6:1–3).

8. Polarity

This philosophical truth involves the recognition that reality is polar, contradictory, ambiguous and paradoxical. In managing severe conflicts it is best not to choose between opposites but to explore the stress inherent in their polarity. As humans, we are both masculine and feminine, destructive and creative, attached and separate, young as well as old. Dealing with such polarities can be a source of deep division in our lives.

It is not possible to solve these paradoxes permanently or

satisfactorily in one direction or another. A solution is constituted and chosen—at a price; for the conflict itself is the truth of existence.[19]

I don't believe that we come to terms with the paradoxical nature of life until we reach middle age. When we are young, with its accompanying idealism, things are seen as black or white. There is right and there is wrong. It is only with maturity that we come to realize that life is just not so simple. There are a great many gray areas.

I found it difficult to understand that I could be very feminine, soft, caring, warm, passive and at the same time very aggressive, self-determined, active, bold, and passionate. I did not have to be one way or the other. The same holds true about issues in life. There is oftentimes more than one correct answer, more than one solution to a dilemma. A crisis oftentimes reveals the contradictory nature about life. This is a difficult truth to grasp because we would much prefer things to be simple. There is tremendous anxiety engendered with the recognition of this philosophical reality but we must come to terms with it if we are to adequately cope with life.

Questions To Ask Ourselves:

1. Would I describe myself as an "all or nothing" kind of person?
2. Do I refuse to make decisions because I don't have the "right" answer?
3. Can I accept the opposite and contradictory aspects of my human nature?
4. Have I made peace with the paradoxical nature of the universe?

Reflect: I will all the more gladly boast of my weaknesses, that the power of Christ may rest upon me. For the sake of Christ, then, I am content with weaknesses ... for when I am weak, then I am strong (2 Cor 12:9–10).

9. Ground, Home, Roots and Foundation

The need for ground or a home is a fact of human existence. In truth, we belong nowhere and we belong everywhere. All homes (family, house, nation, occupation, organization) are only temporary and always questionable.

All "homes" are no more than symbols. Many people feel guilty and bitter because what they thought was a home turned out to be merely ephemeral. Religious tradition is an excellent example of how we express the need to call something our home. Family is another metaphor for home. The human need for an eternal resting place is not found in any of these places. One needs to take responsibility for oneself and not become dependent on a relationship or anything else as an ultimate home.[20]

Anyone who has lost or become separated from his or her family or whose physical house was destroyed or lost due to financial hardship has encountered this truth. Being fired from a job and being excommunicated from a religious tradition are other examples. There are many others. If you allow yourself to go through the pain of such an occurrence you discover the truth that your home is nowhere and yet everywhere. You learn to create your home wherever you are. There is much strength to be gained from such a discovery.

Questions To Ask Ourselves:

1. What does "home" mean to me?
2. Is my personal security dependent on someone or something outside of myself?
3. If I lost my "home" tomorrow, could I cope with that fact?
4. Do I really understand the truth that the only real security is that which I have within myself?

Reflect: Therefore I tell you, do not be anxious about food and drink you need to stay alive, or about clothes for your body. After all, isn't life worth more than food? And isn't the body worth more than clothes? Look at the birds of the air: they neither sow nor reap nor gather into barns, and yet your heavenly Father feeds them. Are you not of more value than they? (Mt 6:25–26).

10. Embodiment

This truth about existence means that we are a body and need to live out our destiny as a body. Embodiment refers to all aspects of physical health. It also means sensitivity to the body's vulnerability. The fear of pain, mutilation, scarring are all expressions of bodily vulnerability.

In the last few years, science has taught us much about illness. We have become aware of the inextricable relationship between mind and body. There is a definite reaction in the body as the result of the thoughts and concerns of the mind. What the mind harbors, the body manifests in some way or another.

It is a proven fact that high levels of stress can have the effect of activating the endocrine system in our bodies with a resulting change in the production of hormones and antibodies. Our natural immune system becomes less effective and our resistance levels are lowered.

There is substantial evidence that the body is greatly affected by emotional distress. Ulcers are not necessarily caused by what you eat but could also be caused by what's eating you. I have seen a number of cases of asthma that appear to be more related to a smothering relationship than to an outside allergen. There is also an apparent link between "bottled-up emotions" and the growth of tumors or other cancer.

All of these facts reminds us that our body is our fundamental home and we must love and care for it. Embodiment is related to the fundamental religious symbol of the incarnation and of the avatar. Embodiment means centeredness in the psychological ego. A crisis that involves our own physical vulnerability or that of a loved one forces us to come to terms with this truth about existence. We are a body and need to live out our life in that body.[21]

Sometimes an illness is a manifestation of the fact that we are not being true to ourselves or that we are not taking our lives seriously. We learn to repress our emotions, and this repression takes its toll on our physical health. We deny our pain, anger, fears, sadness, etc. in the hopes that these emotions will simply disappear. But when emotions are denied they find other avenues for expression. Many people who have life-threatening illnesses discover that a part of their healing involves learning to live honestly and deal with their emotions. They learn that they cannot escape the fact that their bodies are a precious commodity and need to be treated with due respect.

Questions To Ask Ourselves:

1. Do I respect and care for my body?
2. Do I recognize the role emotions play in my physical well-being?
3. What have I done lately to take better care of my body?
4. Do I recognize my bodily limitations?

Reflect: The righteous flourish like the palm tree,
           and grow like a cedar in Lebanon.
      They are planted in the house of the Lord,
           they flourish in the courts of our God.
      They still bring forth fruit in old age,
           they are ever full of sap and green (Ps 92:12–14).

11. The Other and the Reality Principle

This philosophical truth represents the fact that there is something in this world totally different from ourselves that spells out our limitations to us. We all have limitations because we are humans. We can never be perfect no matter how hard we try.

Reality is often difficult to face. Someone has left us or we have failed to pass an important exam. We are all getting older and there is nothing we can do about that fact. These things are essentially inflexible. It is important to recognize that what others do is out of our control. The "other" is a source of frustration, for it can say "no" to us. To grow up is to learn the bitter lessons of reality of the Other and limits to the self.[22]

Many people have a difficult time with this truth. They spend years trying to change others and have a hard time realizing that they just don't have the power to do that. An example is the spouse of the alcoholic who spends all of his or her time trying to keep the spouse from drinking. Programs such as Al-Anon came into existence to help such people learn this principle about "the other." You simply do not have the power to change another. You only have the power to change yourself.

Accepting this philosophical truth about our limitations can really be a freeing experience. Most of us spend the majority of our lives trying to control the uncontrollable. The disease of the 1980's is anxiety disorders. This type of anxiety is not existential in nature but is really neurotic anxiety. It is caused from trying to control what we do not have the power to control due to our human nature. We can't change another person or situation— try as we might—because we are powerless over them. But we can change ourselves—our attitudes and often our own situations. A sense of peace can come from accepting this philosophical truth of human existence.

Questions To Ask Ourselves:

1. Do I respect the freedom of other individuals?
2. Do I have rigid expectations for others?
3. Am I trying to change my loved ones?
4. Am I able to recognize my own limitations?
5. Can I concentrate on my own self-development and let others' development be their own responsibility?

Reflect: God, grant me the serenity to accept the things I cannot
            change, the courage to change the things I can, and the
            wisdom to know the difference.

12. Love and Intimacy

Another truth about human existence is "love" or "encounter." Love is a source of validation. It gives us a feeling of self-
worth and self-esteem as well as making us feel secure, comfortable and at home.

One of the ingredients of love is that all other truths about
existence must be owned and understood. You must be an authentic person in order to have a successful love relationship. It
is the recognition of the philosophical reality that total dependency on another person is an illusion. Neurotic dependency also
violates the philosophical truth of "independent identity." We
must develop ego autonomy or we betray ourselves, which leads
to existential guilt. This leads to self-anger which, when denied,
can be projected onto the partner and be disastrous to our love
relationships.

Another aspect of this truth is the issue of intimacy. This
concept was discussed in depth in Chapter 2. When we are intimate with another, the sense of being an individual consciousness is expanded to the feeling of a communal consciousness. The
spiritual bond between two people who are intimate means that
they can discuss anything no matter now sensitive or delicate.

An additional element of love is engagement. The relationship is real. The partners are committed to each other, and there
is a recognition that the partner is a real person and the self is a
real person. The relationship is a massive exchange of energy.

In order to engage another person we must be willing to
make demands, to confront, and to have the courage to risk saying "no" when it is necessary. In order to do that, we must be
strong enough to tolerate and integrate and learn from a partner's anger, criticism and demands. To love is to make demands
and to have demands made by the partner. Making demands and

confronting are very difficult for most of us. We will stay in unsatisfactory relationships in order to have peace and not have to confront. Having the courage to engage another means we must believe that we are entitled to a healthy relationship.

Love also has the element of partnership. A partnership is able to balance in a mature manner the essential conflicting goals of freedom and intimacy, of separateness and unity, of aloneness and sharing. In other words, love exists when two separate independent freedoms choose to become partners.[23]

> When you ask what love is, you may be too frightened to see the answer.... You may have to shatter the house you have built, you may never go back to the temple.... Fear is not love, nor is love dependence, jealousy, possessiveness, domination, responsibility, duty, self-pity, or any of the other things that conventionally pass for love. If you can eliminate all these, not by forcing them but by washing them away as the rain washes the dust of many days from a leaf, then perhaps you will come upon this strange flower which man always hungers after (Krishnamurti).[24]

Questions To Ask Ourselves:

1. Do I have problems getting close to other people?
2. Do I currently have an intimate relationship in my life?
3. Am I capable of making a commitment to another person?
4. What am I doing today to increase the amount of intimacy in my life?

Reflect: Love is strong as death....
    Its flashes are flashes of fire,
        a most vehement flame.
    Many waters cannot quench love,
        neither can floods drown it (Song 8:6–7).

13. Ethics and Morality

In clinical philosophy we define a healthy person as a person who is also trustworthy, ethical and moral. "An authentic person is one who—regardless of emotions, inclinations or pressures to the contrary—can be trusted to act ethically, morally and in a civilized and democratic manner; it is someone who can be counted on to keep contracts, promises and obligations. An authentic person is honest, lacks duplicity and deceit, does not lie or betray. An authentic person takes pride in being guided by reason and objectivity."[25]

Authenticity is the philosophical word for fulfillment. People are living authentically to the extent to which their lives are in conformity with these truths of human existence. The greater the understanding of these philosophical truths and the more they are integrated into one's life, the more authentic that life will be.

An important distinction between humans and other animals is our moral sense and our understanding of the reality of ethical obligations. Humans have the knowledge of what is right and do not have to merely respond to what gives pleasure. It is human beings alone who are capable of acting on principle.

> Idealism never yet made a person unhappy, grave-faced, and portentiously solemn. It inspires, exhilarates, and gives one a joyful countenance. The person who finds his life's work early, the true course to run, the right mark at which to aim, has a singing heart and a lighthearted step no matter what disasters may overtake him. And the worthier the goal to be won and the higher the purpose to be accomplished, the nobler the harmonies that pour through the soul.[26]

Questions To Ask Ourselves:

1. Can I honestly say that I am an ethical person?
2. Do I live my life in conformity with the philosophical truths of life?

3. If I were to die tomorrow, would I be proud of how I have
   lived my life?

Reflect: If a man is righteous and does what is lawful and right
... does not oppress anyone, but restores to the debtor
his pledge, commits no robbery ... executes true justice
between man and man, walks in my statutes, and is
careful to observe my ordinances—he is righteous (Ez
18:5, 7–9).

The Importance of the Philosophical Truths

I have summarized some of the major truths of existence
but there are others. All of these truths are described in full in
Koestenbaum's writings. The principal truths that I have con-
centrated on here are anthropological or psychological. These are
the basic existential issues. There is a second set of tenets or truths
which are metaphysical, religious and ontological. These are referred to as the transpersonal issues and are to be confronted only
after all of the existential issues have been thoroughly worked
through. Basic matters like earning a living, raising a family, getting an education, etc. must be taken care of before we can contemplate the mystical possibilities of existence.

The metaphysical truths are for the winter of life—after the
issues to which the psychological truths address themselves have
been worked through. If you reverse the process you are in danger of using the metaphysical issues as a way of denying the importance of the psychological truths.[27]

Most mystics understand that you cannot give something up
until you have achieved something. In other words, ego bound-
aries must be hardened before they can be softened. You must
have developed an individual identity before you can transcend
it. One must find oneself before one can lose oneself.

You simply cannot become involved with the ascetic or
mystical world until you have learned what it means to be a hu-

man being in this world. The majority of us have hardly touched these existential issues and are guilty of using religion or spirituality as a means of escaping their painful reality. It is extremely important that we not allow ourselves to evade the existential philosophical truths about human existence.

It is the belief of clinical philosophy that access to these truths is the secret of authenticity and fulfillment. Health means to live in conformity with these important facts of life. Again, the greater we understand them and the more we integrate them into our lives, the more authentic and healthy we will be. If we don't integrate these truths into our life we will continue to experience symptoms.

Experiencing any or all of these philosophical truths provides us with the realization that we are contacting something deep inside us which is really part of the universal cosmos. It is possible to think of any one of these truths as the most important or the more central one. All of them are equally important. Each one must be considered with a high degree of seriousness as if it appears to be the only one that matters.

A severe crisis will reveal usually one central theme—a philosophical truth which appears to stand out. It may be freedom when we are faced with an important, critical decision. It may be death if we are facing a serious illness. It may be aloneness when we are betrayed or abandoned. It sometimes is useful to select one as the most basic at a particular time and see the others as supporting it.

All of these truths are organically related. All must be fulfilled or realized in order to live a symptom-free life. You need all of them. They must be integrated into your life in order to live authentically. A crisis provides us with an excellent opportunity to learn these painful as well as life-enhancing truths.

Learning about these philosophical truths of human existence helped me tremendously during many painful times. Something deep inside of me recognized that there were many lessons about life that I had previously failed to learn. I also knew instinctively that these were things I needed to know if I was to grow. When you are in a state of intense pain, you are so open and very raw. It is a time when new insights can find their way inside us. It is a time when we must question our previous assumptions about life and the way things "ought to be." I really believe that the Lord sometimes takes us into troubled waters *not* to drown us, but to cleanse us.

Philosophy helped me make a friend of pain and enabled me to cope during some very trying times. Ever since I was a little girl, I had always questioned life. I was never one to accept things blindly. I was a very quiet child but, at the same time, very deep. I always would say to myself when puzzled by life: "But it doesn't have to be that way! There has to be another answer!" I did not know that this was the voice of a survivor, the voice of my soul. Philosophy has given me many of the answers that I was seeking. And finding these answers has given me peace.

How does the soul grow? Not all in a minute;
Now it may lose ground, and now it may win it;
Now it resolves, and again the will faileth;
Now it rejoiceth, and now it bewaileth;
Now its hopes fructify, and then they are blighted;
Now it walks sullenly, now gropes benighted;
Fed by discouragements, taught by disaster;
So it goes forward, now slower, now faster,
Till all the pain is past, and failure made whole,
It is full grown, and the Lord rules the soul.
(Susan Coolidge)[28]

Chapter 4

———— • ————

Crisis: Getting Through
the Pain

Talking about what we should learn from a crisis is rela-
tively easy. We can intellectualize about this and it sounds like
something we can handle. The going gets much tougher when
we are actually in the throes of a crisis. Mere intellectualizing
isn't much help then. There is nothing worse in the world than
to be in emotional pain. Physical pain appears to be more bear-
able. You can call on medications to assist you in dealing with
the pain. But that is not so with emotional pain. You may be able
to drug yourself so that you lose consciousness, but you must
wake up sometime and the pain is still there.

So how do we deal with this kind of pain? And what do
we do about the fears that such pain evokes? How do we handle
the confrontation with pure, unadulterated evil that crisis situations reveal? Lets take a look at these issues in detail.

Dealing with Emotional Pain

As a child, I was very afraid of physical pain, yet I should
have been much more afraid of emotional pain. But children do
not comprehend such distinctions. I just knew that I couldn't
survive any kind of pain, and that is why I prayed so fervently
that God would spare me such experiences.

It is almost humorous to me now when I reflect back on
this time. What a ridiculous prayer! Even if God had the desire
to stop crises from coming into my life, my growth would have

been stunted had he granted my wish. What I should have prayed for was the strength to survive the pain. That would have been a legitimate request.

What I did not understand as a child was the fact that there can be no growth without pain. Furthermore, the level of growth is proportionate to the amount of the pain. So the more pain you can endure, the better off you are. Real and lasting growth requires unbearable pain. There is no side-stepping this fact.

We experience emotional pain whenever we are in a crisis. Something of value has been destroyed. It could be the loss of children, family, or a marriage. It could also be the loss of hopes, health or ideals. The destruction is irreversible and forever. The loss can never again be recovered and the memories will continue on. I had a dream of the family and marriage that I wanted. That particular dream was lost to me forever. It has taken me many years to recover from that loss.

Emotional pain is also caused from the fact that we have made certain choices in our lives that led to that particular crisis. In some situations, we really did it to ourselves. A great deal of guilt results from such a realization. We could have been wiser, smarter or more courageous. We could have been better at prioritizing our values. I kept telling myself that if I had waited to get married until I was older and more mature, it would have worked out differently. I went through a stage where I was incredibly hard on myself. My pain was so intense that when I couldn't find anyone or anything else to blame I started in on myself. It took a long time to get to the place where I forgave myself. I finally came to the realization and to accepting the fact that I am not perfect. I have flaws and limitations, and that is O.K. I am human, and humans make mistakes.

I also came to realize that whenever I risk moving toward another person, there is always the risk that that person will move away from me, leaving me painfully alone. The price of loving is pain because anything that is alive will die. But if I refuse to risk pain, then I must be willing to live without many things that make life meaningful and worthwhile.

Pain as well as joy is the result of growing and moving forward in life. Therefore, a full life will be full of pain. The only alternative is not to live fully or not to live at all. If I elect life and growth, then I also elect change and the prospect of death. These are truths about life that I have learned to accept and I no longer question.

But what about the pain? How do we get through that part? I will share with you what I now know to be true. Because I can now say that I have been "schooled" in pain, I believe that I can teach others. But really, the only way to learn how to survive pain is the actual experience of doing so. I can really only represent the fact that such pain is survivable. I, as well as others, am living testimony to the fact that it is possible to survive unbearable pain.

When the emotional pain first hits, it is quite common to go into shock. Our natural defenses kick in to temporarily protect us. You often see people whose loved one has died looking almost calm at the funeral. They are still in shock. The painful time comes when the shock wears off. While in this initial period of shock, you walk around emotionally dead. You go through all the necessary motions but you are not really there. You become disorganized and disoriented. You have no appetite and you have problems falling asleep. When you are finally able to fall asleep, you are absolutely exhausted. This is a time when you really need a good support system around you.

After the shock wears off you find yourself experiencing the pain. This is pure, unadulterated pain. Your emotions are raw. You cry all the time. This is the time to just let yourself *feel* to the depth of your being. When I was experiencing this stage, I would lie down, put my arms around myself and just rock myself back and forth. This was my way of comforting myself. I would say soothing words like "It's going to be all right, Anita" or "You will be O.K." and just let the tears flow. There were times when

I would just sob to the depth of my being—heart-wrenching sobs. The process of doing so was utterly exhausting.

There was a point at which I would have done anything to stop the pain. It felt so horrible. It felt as if it would never end. The only way I felt I could end it was by suicide. When I was actually at the point of considering suicide I felt absolutely hopeless. I was in utter despair. I felt as if even God had abandoned me. I was screaming out from the core of my being, "Please, God, stop this pain. I can't bear much more of this." And just at the point when the pain was at its worst, when I was feeling the most desolate, some small glimmer of hope came into my consciousness. Maybe, I thought to myself, just maybe, the future holds something positive. Maybe life will get better. Just maybe. It was at that point that I experienced the ground.

Going through this experience is like falling into a deep dark pit. You keep falling and falling, deeper and deeper. I cannot adequately describe to you what it feels like. But at that moment where a glimmer of hope came to my consciousness, I felt the ground again. It is really a death–rebirth experience. At the point that I felt that ground, I began to come back up again. I really believe that the ground I am referring to is "God." And that is what resurrection is really all about.

This experience is a very personal one but has been collaborated by others. Each person's experience of this rebirth process may be somewhat different. But all who have experienced it state that you must move down and backward before you can move up and forward. In other words, you must go down before you can come up. If people get stuck in this process and become depressed, it may well be that they have not gone down far enough. You must go down to the point where you find ground before true transformation can take place. The problem is that when you are in the process of falling into this pit of darkness, you are not sure there will be a ground. It takes Faith to believe that the ground will be there.

When I got to the place where a glimmer of hope came into

my consciousness, I made an existential decision to say "yes" to life. I was not aware of doing that at the time, but as I reflect back on it, that is exactly what I was doing. I chose to believe that life would get better and that it was worth the gamble to go on.

What I have just described to you is what is meant by the term "existential crisis" that I referred to in Chapter 3. As I allowed myself to fall into that abyss of anxiety, that pit of total aloneness, I was experiencing human reality. I was able to take it. I never before believed I could survive such pain. And just when the pain got intolerable I found my ground. I did validate myself and existentially chose to make a commitment to myself by saying "yes" to life. I cannot express to you the kind of strength this experience has given me. I now know that I can take anything that life deals out. I certainly am not looking forward to any more crises in my life, but I now know for a fact that *I can take it,* should it ever happen again. And it will happen again. I am not naive the way I was as a little girl. But just knowing that I can survive has transformed my fear into courage.

I suppose it would be convenient if there was a pill for instant strength. I could make a fortune selling that pill. Unfortunately, strength is built layer by layer. Each layer is inevitably composed, at least in part, of wounds, failures and losses. It takes strength to risk loss. But each time you go through this process it becomes easier. It is like training for a sport or practicing a musical instrument—we get better with time.

When you are in the stage of dealing with the emotional pain, other people can't help you. It is a solitary journey. It is important to know that there are others standing by when you start the journey back up again. But during the time that you are in the deepest pain, there is the belief that no one can be of help. You are very much in touch with the existential truth of human aloneness. You feel so utterly abandoned. No one can comfort you. You have to do that for yourself.

When I was at that point in my own crisis, the comfort of

someone else's arms would not have helped. What I needed to learn was how to comfort myself. I had to learn to rely on the comfort of my own arms around me. And that comfort had to be enough.

If you have never experienced what I am saying, it may sound strange or maybe even crazy. Picturing a grown woman, with her arms around herself, rocking herself in a fetal position, seems rather bizarre. But that is truly a rebirth experience. It was a way of making an unconditional commitment to myself, the only kind of unconditional commitment that there is. Each of us must do this in our own way. That was mine.

I have learned that in the solitude of grieving, you need to find courage to trust your God-given emotional and physiological processes that allow for full and honest expression of inner pain. That can be accomplished through crying, moaning, trembling, or shaking. One of the unfortunate ways that this natural healing is blocked is by responding to the cultural message that says crying is a sign of weakness. As Anne Morrow Lindbergh so wisely states: "Grief is the great leveler.... Stoicism ... is only a halfway house.... It is a shield, permissible for a short time only. In the end one has to discard shields and remain open and vulnerable. Otherwise, scar tissue will seal off the wound and no growth will follow. To grow, to be reborn, one must remain vulnerable—open to love but also hideously open to the possibility of more suffering."[1]

If the natural grieving process is blocked, there can be no psychological "closure" on the situation. The psychological wound cannot heal. If we are to get back in touch with life, we must give in to the profound feelings of hurt and pain as the flood of emotional energy is discharged. When we can give vent to hurt feelings, we are able to see things in a new way. We can finally accept what has happened, take the losses realistically, and move on. Having had the courage to give up a fanatical hold on how things "should have been," we now are able to regain touch with events, relationships and circumstances that are currently emerging in our lives. In this way we gain closure on the situation.

Learning to accept pain and sorrow is a lifelong process and very much a part of life. We each intuitively know that we have our own important lessons to learn. This point is well illustrated in the following:

> The Hasidic Jews have a story about the Sorrow Tree. According to them, on Judgment Day, each person will be invited to hang from the Tree of Sorrows all of his own miseries, and that done, he will be given permission to walk around the tree and survey everyone else's miseries in order to select a set he likes better. According to Hasidic legend, each person then freely chooses his own personal set of sorrows once more.[2]

This story is a poignant reminder that no one lives a pain-free life. Other people's sorrows nearly always look worse to us than our own. We hear stories about what other people have endured and we say to ourselves "I could never have survived that." When we hear about a tragedy that has befallen someone else, we glance toward heaven, thanking God that it was not us.

We all need to become better at pain management. One important thing that I have learned from my own experience and from counseling others is that something beneficial can come from having setbacks or failures at an early age. We need to teach our children that broken hearts, like broken bones, heal with time, if we will just let them.

Rabbi Kushner talks about the kind of people that most of us grew up envying, who appeared to live charmed lives. Everything seemed to go so smoothly for them. What is interesting is that it never occurred to us that living a life of constant pleasure sets one up for a life of frustration afterward. Kushner points out that there are skills that are not acquired and habits that are not formed. There are lessons not learned about the real world during those years of having everything go smoothly. I would heartily agree with him that such people never learn the important lessons of patience, hard work and tolerance for failure in themselves and others. They have not learned the discipline of patience and how to postpone gratification. They are unprepared for the day when a crisis hits and the reality of the real world confronts them.[3]

In my previous book *Mothers Are People Too*, I talked extensively about the negative aspects of being too protective of our children. We need to give them the freedom to make their own mistakes and learn from them. If we do everything for them, using as the excuse that we are being good mothers, we do them a disservice. We can be far better parents by giving our children permission to fail. Learning early that you can survive defeat makes you tougher and more resilient for the rest of your life.

I think that I would have been better off if I had experienced more losses and setbacks in my earlier years. Perhaps my fear of pain would have been lessened. I think that my crisis period in my thirties was more intense because I had not confronted some of these developmental or philosophical issues at an earlier age. I would remind myself that I was "a little late and slightly breathless" in my development but "better late than never." I am sure that having more experience in dealing with pain at an earlier age would have been helpful.

Confronting Fear

As I mentioned in Chapter 1, there are two kinds of crisis. Type I crises are maturational ones and more subtle. Type II crises are those that happen by accident such as a death of a loved one or a serious illness. My crises were more Type II in nature although there were certainly maturational elements involved also. Type II crises hit you over the head. You are forced to deal with them in some fashion. Type I can be avoided by repressing the anxiety that is signaling the need to make a change.

Lets take for an example a woman, age forty, who is very unhappy with her life. She has raised several children but still feels lacking because she has let others dominate her and keep her from pursuing her own goals. She has tried many tactics over the years, including fighting, pouting, or keeping silent. It was certainly possible for her to find the power to make changes in her life, even in basic ways. But in order to do so, she would have to give up her fears and helplessness. The key turning point for her was only going to come when she was finally able to admit a deep desire to make something out of her life and express a willingness to face her many fears. Among her fears was that she was too old to find an occupation, that her marriage would dissolve, that her children would reject her, and that no one would like her.

Fear is the reason so many people get stuck in life and stop growing. Everyone experiences fear. It is how we handle the fear that is so important. Do we use the fear as a catalyst for growth, or do we become paralyzed by it?

Human beings need to be loved, and when they are not loved, they experience great pain, hurt and fear. In order to survive, a person may adopt a specific defensive stance in life rather than dare spontaneous expression and risk being hurt again. One literally gets scared out of being oneself.

If you are experiencing a maturation type crisis, you are not absolutely forced to make any changes. You are aware that life has lost its direction or meaning but you may not be miserable enough to do anything about it. This is where a massive dose of pain can be helpful. I always tell people that no one comes into therapy voluntarily unless he or she is in pain. The degree of pain has much to do with a person's motivation to change.

Defenses are learned strategies; we are not born with them. Once we discover how we make ourselves tense, rigid, and controlled in our posture toward life, we can begin to reverse the process. But the process of growing out of our psychological rut is not without risk and pain.

A strong feeling of fear, anxiety, hostility, guilt, or depression may be a signpost that indicates that one has gotten off the track. If one becomes aware of these feelings, and exercises the courage to look for new and different options, then growth can be restored and one is back on the path of healthy living again.

It is my belief that you can postpone maturational or developmental crises but you pay a tremendous price. The problems don't disappear; they just increase. As I mentioned in my previous book *Seasons: Woman's Search for Self Through Life's Stages*, avoiding necessary developmental issues only succeeds in making later stages more problematic. You may think you are successfully avoiding problems, but you are not. They will come back to haunt you and your existential guilt will have increased because of the years that you have wasted.

Life is like a seed growing into a tree in that it unfolds stage by stage.

> Triumphant ascent, collapse, crises, failures, and new beginnings strew the way. It is the path trodden by the great majority of mankind, as a rule unreflectingly, unconsciously, unsuspectingly, following its labyrinthine windings from birth to death in hope and longing. It is hedged about with struggle and suffering, joy and sorrow, guilt and error, and nowhere is there security from catastrophe. For as soon as a man tries to escape every risk and prefers to experience life only in his head, in the form of ideas and fantasies, as soon as he surrenders to opinions of "how it ought to be" and, in order not to make a false step, imitates others whenever possible, he forfeits the chance of his own independent development. Only if he treads the path bravely and flings himself into life, fearing no struggle and no exertion and fighting shy of no experience, will he mature his personality more fully than the man who is ever trying to keep to the safe side of the road.[4]

I agree with Jolande Jacobi that in view of these high demands, it is not surprising that the majority of people follow the path of least resistance and confine themselves to the fulfillment of biological and material needs. They look toward gaining the greatest possible number of pleasurable experiences. Most people look unremittingly for happiness in all the wrong places. It never occurs to them that happiness is not the goal of life set for them by the Creator. The true goal is a task that continues right up till the end of life, namely, the most complete and comprehensive development of the personality. It is this which gives life an incomparable value that can never be lost: inner peace, and therewith the highest form of happiness.[5]

I think that once you realize the truth of what I am saying, you will find the courage to risk making changes. I, for one, used to be very afraid of taking any risks. But now I now realize that the other side of fear is excitement. And risking can be very exciting. Now that I can see the positive side to taking risks I am no longer afraid of making changes or trying new things. I have become addicted to wanting to grow and be all that I can be.

There is a wonderful fairy tale by the Brothers Grimm entitled "The Tale of the One Who Went Forth to Learn Fear" that has a very relevant message.

Once upon a time, there was a young boy who, no matter what he did, never felt afraid. He felt incomplete without the emotional dimension of fear. So he went out and had many hair-raising adventures, encountered ghosts and witches and fire-breathing dragons, but never felt even a shudder. In his last adventure, he freed a castle from a wicked spell, and in gratitude the king gave him his daughter in marriage. The hero told his bride that, although he was fond of her, he was not sure he could marry her until he completed his mission of learning to feel fear. On their wedding night, his wife pulled back the covers and threw a bucket of cold water full of little fish over him. He cried out, "Oh my dear wife, now I know what it is to shudder," and he was happy.[6]

In this story, the hero cannot feel love or joy until he is able to feel fear and dread. He is not really grown up and ready for adult life until he becomes emotionally mature and open to feeling. This hero can be a symbol to us all that if we attempt to avoid being hurt by deadening ourselves to all feeling, we will miss out on a lot of positive aspects of life.[7] It all comes back to the fact that there will be no song on our lips if there is never any anguish in our hearts. Joy and sorrow are two sides of the same coin. There is no evading this truth if we are to grow.

It is extremely important that we remember that the deepest urge or instinct within every living creature is to fulfill itself. In human life this urge toward fulfillment does not come from our conscious minds, but from the unconscious Center of our being, the Self. Fulfillment is thus urged upon us from within. The fulfillment of our being requires the forging of a unified personality, in which the conscious mind and the unconscious mind are acting in unison and not in opposition to each other. Carl Jung has called the lifelong process that aims at fulfillment "individuation," since in this process an indivisible, undivided personality is the goal. In other words, fulfillment can only come when the conscious personality expresses in a unified life as completely as possible the totality of the personality, most of which, to begin with, is unknown to us.[8] Growth is simply not possible without risk. And fear is always a companion to risk.

The Problem of Evil

I don't think that it is possible to write a book on crisis and not have to discuss the issue of evil. We run right into evil in times of crisis. It could be the evil in the world, in other people, or in ourselves. But the fact is that evil is a part of life, and at some point we will have to come to terms with this fact.

It is important that we begin to understand the role that evil plays in our lives. The hardest fact to accept is that there is the potential for evil in all of us. According to William Miller, movement toward the achievement of wholeness or completeness is accomplished not only through the continued infusion of goodness, righteousness, and morality but also through the acceptance and conscious incorporation of one's dark and shadowy side into oneself. We are not complete until we incorporate into our conscious self that dark side of our person which is every bit as much a part of us as is that bright self which we parade before the world.[9]

As Christians, we are rather reluctant to accept the fact that we are capable of great good as well as great evil. We hesitate to deal with this concept because it may appear to be "courting the devil." The thought of taking something of dark or negative quality and incorporating it constructively into our life is very threatening. In actual experience it is the opposite that is true. It is the person who repeatedly denies and represses his dark side who is much more vulnerable to its power and much more likely to be overcome by it than is the person who learns how to use this dark side constructively.[10]

What we need to remember and remind ourselves of is the fact that individuation is the process whereby a person becomes in the truest sense what he or she in fact is. As we develop psychologically, we come to identify with our ego ideal and reject all those qualities that contradict it. But the rejected qualities do not cease to exist simply because they have been denied direct expression. Instead they live on within us and form the secondary personality that psychology calls the Shadow.

The Shadow is like a foreign personality—a primitive, instinctive, animalistic kind of being. It is the collection of uncivilized desires and feelings that simply have no place in cultured society. The shadow is everything we don't want to be. Or rather it is perhaps everything we would like to be but don't dare. The shadow is everything we don't want others to know about us. It is everything we don't want to know about ourselves and have thus conveniently "forgotten" through denial and repression. The concept of the "Shadow" is aptly revealed in the following:

There is a sixth-century Indian legend about a scorpion and a tortoise who were facing a swollen river, and the scorpion begged the tortoise to carry him across. "I can't take you on my back," the tortoise replied. "You'd sting me."

"Why would I do that?" the scorpion wanted to know. "You'd be my life raft. If I stung you we'd both drown."

"Well," said the tortoise, "since you put it that way, I guess it'll be all right. Hop on."

So the scorpion climbed on the tortoise's back and they set out across the river, and when they were almost to the shore, the scorpion stung the tortoise, and as they were both going down, the tortoise turned to the scorpion and asked: "Just tell me this, before we drown. Why did you do it? I have to know."

And the scorpion replied, looking perhaps a little regretful, "What can I tell you? I couldn't help myself. It's my nature."[11]

That little scorpion could have been any one of us. One of the most common mistakes we make is to believe that we have successfully gotten rid of all our primitive savagery. In fact, all that has happened is that it has been successfully repressed into the unconscious where it resides as vitally as ever. We all keep stored away in our Shadows the multitude of qualities and dynamics that we would like to pretend do not exist.[12] We simply refuse to recognize the fact that human beings are capable of great good, but the opposite always will reside within our Shadow. Each of us is also capable of horrendous evil. We often run right into this reality during a crisis.

This fact makes it very important that we remind ourselves that the goal of life is completion and not perfection. If a man thinks that he can actually be perfect, that is, become like God, life will again and again bring about his downfall. All of us must constantly run up against our limits lest we become too arrogant.

We may strive after perfection but must suffer from the opposite of our intentions for the sake of our completeness. As Jung states: "There is no light without shadow and no psychic wholeness without imperfection. To round itself out, life calls not for perfection but for completeness; and for this the 'thorn in the flesh' is needed, the suffering of defects without which there is no progress and no ascent."[13]

In order to become "whole," all the various parts of us must perform their proper function, and the proper function of the ego includes becoming conscious, that is, psychologically enlightened and aware. Few people become conscious without *having* to become conscious, without being driven to it by necessity. This is where evil comes in. It is only when people encounter evil in some form—as pain, loss of meaning, or something that appears to be threatening or destructive to them—that they begin to find their way to consciousness. Only when people are tested in the fire of life, so that what is weak within them is purged away and only the strong elements remain, does individuation take place. And this purging can only take place in the context of a certain amount of suffering and struggle. Paradoxically, without a power in life that seems to oppose wholeness, the achievement of wholeness would be impossible. Therefore, evil becomes a necessity if individuation is to occur.[14]

Since the psyche is built on polar opposites which complement each other, but also stand in glaring contradiction to each other, it must of its very nature exist in a state of tension and suffer this. It can even be said that the confrontation with these opposites lies at the heart of the individuation process. To be "whole" means, at the same time, to be full of contradictions.[15]

We need to accept the fact that there is good and evil in all of us. Any of us who wishes to have an answer to the problem of evil has a need for self-knowledge first. We must understand and recognize how much good we can do, and what crimes we are capable of. Both elements are within our nature, and both are bound to come to light in us.

One can neither act out nor consciously deny evil. We must admit that no human life can entirely escape it. Oftentimes we make monumental efforts to keep only the good, the permitted thoughts and feelings in our consciousness. We attempt to exclude the numerous drives and qualities which belong to our "nonangelic" side. We do not want to admit them to ourselves or to others. That is why we become panicky and fearful or defensive whenever the slightest criticism puts our allegedly angelic side in question. "To know that evil ever dwells within us, to learn to bear this knowledge instead of foisting it off on other people and always blaming them for everything, is one of the most important postulates of individuation."[16]

According to Jacobi, peace is found only at the center of the two poles—the light and the dark. At that midpoint one can be wholly human, neither angel nor devil, but simply human, partaker of both worlds. "The search for this center, for this balance of the soul is a lifelong undertaking. It is the basic task and the ultimate goal of psychotherapy. For this center is also the place where the Divine filters through into the Soul and reveals itself in the God-images, in the Self."[17]

The "balance" that Jacobi is referring to is the state in which both worlds, the light and the dark, the good and the bad, the joyful and the sorrowful, are united in self-evident acceptance and reflect the true nature of man's inborn duality. This individuation process therefore leads to the highest possible development and completeness of the psychic personality and in a preparation for the end of life.[18]

When we are experiencing a crisis, we often come face to face with pure, unadulterated evil. We are being exposed to the dark side of life. The evil may be death, disease, or a natural disaster such as an earthquake or a forest fire. I personally believe that the hardest evil of all to deal with is people's inhumanity to others. This is an example of the

Shadow side of the personality gone beserk. A crisis often exposes us to this kind of evil. To make some kind of peace with evil, to learn to confront it in ourselves and in others, is a monumental challenge and takes tremendous courage. What stance should we take when confronted with this kind of evil? Perhaps, Madame Chiang Kai-shek, the First Lady of China, put it best when she said:

> If the past has taught us anything it is that every cause brings its effect, every action has a consequence. We Chinese have a saying: "If a man plants melons he will reap melons; if he sows beans, he will reap beans." And this is true of everyone's life; good begets good, and evil leads to evil.
>
> True enough, the sun shines on the saint and the sinner alike, and too often it seems that the wicked prosper. But we can say with certainty that with the individual as with the nation, the flourishing of the wicked is an illusion, for, unceasingly, life keeps books on us all.
>
> In the end, we are all the sum total of our actions. Character cannot be counterfeited, nor can it be put on and cast off as if it were a garment to meet the whim of the moment. Like the markings on wood which are ingrained in the very heart of the tree, character requires time and nurturing for growth and development.
>
> Thus also, day by day, we write our own destiny; for inexorably ... we become what we do.[19]

To be able to accept the fact that there is evil in all of us does not give us permission to act it out. The goal of human development is to make friends with your Shadow; for we achieve good not apart from evil, but through it, even in spite of it.[20] We need to learn to say to our Shadow, "Yes, my Shadow, I acknowledge you and your power as a part of me, and I respect the magnitude of that power. But I will not forget, nor will you, Shadow, that the power of light is greater than the power of darkness."[21]

Sometimes, in order to take a stand against evil, we are forced to call forth our own Shadow, or dark side. We may have to fight for our lives in ways we never would under normal circumstances. Now we need to be in touch with our Shadow. The power contained in the Shadow can save us. It never occurs to us that the personality characteristics that are contained in the Shadow are those characteristics that make us most alive, vital and self-determined. People who have stood up to evil and assessed the Shadow side of their personality have a certain gleam or sparkle in their eye. This sparkle gives them "true grit" and is an invaluable commodity. It is the coming face to face with evil during a crisis situation that results in the development of this particular kind of strength. And this is a type of strength that can never be lost.

It is our responsibility to learn how both to fight evil and to learn from it. "We resist it, but we use it for good. We are to take that which may appear to be undesirable, unacceptable, and even objectionable and use it positively, constructively, and even creatively, thus bringing ourselves closer towards wholeness and completion. This, in fact, is our task!"[22]

> "Remember," said Jesus, "I am sending you out like sheep among wolves: so be cunning as serpents and yet harmless as doves" (Mt 10:16).

The Importance of the Pain

There is a great deal involved in the process of getting through the pain of a crisis. The possibility of a personal transformation is certainly present. The individuation process can be furthered during this difficult time. Rebirth becomes possible with every "death." And a crisis is a death. Most people, however, prefer to be born only once. They are afraid of the pains without which there can be no birth. They have no trust in the natural striving of the psyche toward its goal. And so there are all too many who halt on life's way. They venture nothing; they would rather forego the prize. Many of us never seem to understand that the greatest problems in life can never be finally solved. As Jung so well states, "The meaning and purpose of a problem seem to lie not in its solution but in our working at it incessantly."

Getting through the pain of a crisis does take courage. You have to be willing to endure the pain, confront your worst fears, and deal with the issue of evil. A crisis can move us further down the road to individuation, if we will just let it. There is so very much to be gained from a crisis. It is a real pity whenever we waste these opportunities to grow. If I, who was one of the world's biggest cowards, can survive such an experience, then so can you. The human spirit is capable of enduring much more than we think.

There is an apocryphal story about a man who turned to God one night when he was sorely tried and called out, "When can I stop giving, God? I haven't anything more to give!"

"You can stop giving when I stop giving to you," came the answer.

"When you stop giving to me!" the man cried out, enraged, thinking of his son who was fatally ill and his ex-wife who made his life miserable, and even of his friends who loved him but could do nothing for him in his pain— and only stood by feeling impotent, or worse ran from him out of weakness and fright and had to be consoled. "All you are giving me is pain and sorrow."

"No, that isn't right," came the answer. "I gave you life, and that is my gift, a pearl of great price. The pain and sorrow are another matter. But since you brought them up, they have made you a strong man, don't you agree? Would you rather be a weaker man, perhaps a man like one of your friends who is less certain of his strength because he has always been given to?"

"Since you put it that way," said the man, feeling chastened, "I would like to thank you for the gift of my life and for helping me develop the strength to be a giver. I realize now that it is a privilege to be able to give and will complain no more."[23]

Chapter 5

Surviving a Crisis

How is it that some people are so able to survive adversity? Such people seem able to roll with whatever punches life deals them. When faced with crises and problems in their personal lives, they take the risk of making inner changes. They understand and accept that life crises are inevitable.

Gail Sheehy, in her book *Pathfinders*, describes such people as persons of high well-being. High well-being appears to be the result of having made many of the right choices and having emphasized the right personality characteristics. By setting out with optimism, anticipating the future, finding meaning and direction in their lives, and pursuing these cheerfully, rarely slowing down over disappointments and not allowing themselves to be set back by others' criticism, these people established a forward momentum that carried them through life.[1]

High well-being people all had the following characteristics in common. They are listed in order of importance.

1. Their lives had meaning and direction.

2. They have experienced one or more important transitions in their adulthood and handled these transitions in an unusual, personal, or creative way.

3. They rarely felt cheated or disappointed in life. They may have experienced numerous setbacks but never allowed these to deter them or make them bitter. Instead, they learned from them and made the necessary changes that would enable them to move on.

4. They have already attained several of the long-term goals that were important to them.

5. They reported being pleased with their personal growth and development.[2]

People of high well-being reported that they got their sense of well-being from having successfully dealt with a failure or loss. Roughly half of all the people who scored high on well-being admitted to having "failed" at a major personal or professional endeavor but almost every one of them had the same response. They found it a useful experience and say that they are better off because of it. "What they did was learn from the experience. In the process they were strengthened. Their resiliency in failure does not make them immune. They feel the blows—often severely. It is just that they don't go down for the count or retire in fear from the fray. Knowing that one has survived a failure adds to the armor needed during times of risk, transition and uncertainty ahead."[3]

As Hans Selye so well puts it "It is not what happens that matters but how you take it." Resiliency in failure and the ability to survive crises are not qualities with which one is born. They are acquired strengths. One cannot acquire expertise without experience. Every problem can teach us something. We can learn, change and grow.

What are the characteristics of a survivor? How do people survive adversity? Robert Veninga, in his book entitled *The Book of Hope*, describes the common characteristics needed in order to survive a crisis.

Characteristic 1: If you want to survive a tragedy you need a friend.

Almost without exception those who survive a tragedy give credit to one person who stood by them and were a source of support. Their supporters gave them a sense of hope. Kahlil Gibran once remarked that we can forget those with whom we have laughed, but we can never forget those with whom we have cried. Most friendships worth their salt are those nourished in human struggle. Once you have suffered together, there is a bond that is not severed by the passage of time.

Good friendships help us cope with our most terrifying fears. Being vulnerable masks a more basic fear. The most primal fear of all is the "threat of abandonment." It is learned at birth. A friendship affirms that we will not be abandoned.[4]

There were a number of friends who stood by me during my own personal crises. One such friend was a tremendous support for me when I was going through my divorce. Her name was Marge. Because she was older and much more experienced in life, she had much wisdom from which I benefited immensely. I could call her anytime and, no matter what emotion I was feeling at the time, she would listen and validate my experience. When I needed to get angry but was too afraid of that emotion to get in touch with it, she would get angry for me.

As I mentioned earlier, I am a very sensitive individual and I was taking everything that was happening to me very personally. My self-esteem and self-confidence were therefore at all-time lows. But Marge knew just what to say to me to help me see things objectively and not to blame myself for everything that transpired. She stood by me and was an invaluable ally. She represented reality and sanity at a time when everything in my life was in a state of chaos. I will be eternally grateful to Marge.

I always felt badly because I was never able to repay Marge for the support she had given me. She never, while I knew her, was in a position to need that same kind of support from me. I know she had a lot of sadness and loss in her life but it happened before I had met her. Someone else had been there for her just as she had been there for me.

I look at such incidents of support as part of a "master plan." It's as if there is a giant bank account in the sky. And when you need support, you withdraw from it, and when times are better, you add to this account by being there for someone else. I never was able to give back to Marge directly, but I gave to many other people in their personal times of need. I paid back the loan. What is important is that we remember to pay back such loans and to also be willing to withdraw support from this account whenever necessary. Every one of us will at some time need a Marge.

> The job of a friend is not to decide what should be done, not to run interference or pick up the slack. The job of a friend is to understand, and to supply energy and hope, and in doing so to keep those they value on their feet a little longer, so that they can fight another round and grow stronger in themselves.[5]

Characteristic 2: Those who survive a tragedy understand the magnitude of that which they have lost.

If you want to recover from a crisis, you need to enter fully into your tragedy. You need to feel in the depth of your being what it is that you have lost. Human pain does not let go of its grip at one point in time. Rather, it works its way out of our consciousness over time. There is a season of sadness. A season of anger. A season of tranquillity. A season of Hope.[6]

There is a process in grieving. Dr. Kübler-Ross, in her work with dying patients, found that there were five stages in the process of dying. These stages can be generalized to other crisis states as well. People do not necessarily experience all the stages, nor do these stages occur in a fixed or orderly sequence. Kübler-Ross' work is very useful for sensitizing us to some of the major issues and problems that we must face when we are grieving over a loss.[7] The stages in the grief process are as follows:

1. Denial: Typically denial is expressed with, "No, not me," on becoming aware of the loss. We may deny even when we are told the facts explicitly. Denial is necessary as a delaying mechanism so that we can absorb the reality of our situation. During this phase, we may wish to remain in isolation and may also refuse to talk. Pressing a person to acknowledge and accept a bitter reality before he or she is psychologically ready or able can reinforce the need for defensive denial.

2. Anger: When denial finally gives way, it is often replaced by anger. "Why me?" We may express anger by making

accusations against the people who are trying to help. We are angry because other people's lives seem so much better. We are really angry at fate, or God, but often take it out on those closest to us. This anger needs to be expressed and will pass.

3. Bargaining: With the evidence that the crisis is still there in spite of angry protests about this fact, we may in effect say, "Maybe if I ask nicely, I'll be heard." This is the stage of bargaining. The bargaining goes on mostly with God, even among those who don't believe in God. Bargaining consists usually of private promises: "I'll live a good life," or "I'll donate my life, my money to a great cause." During this phase there may be underlying feelings of guilt or regrets. We really need someone who can listen to these expressions of regret.

4. Depression: During this stage of grieving we will probably become depressed. Our initial anger may be turned inward. We need supportive friends to just be with us during this time. If the depression does not lift within a reasonable period of time (approximately six months), professional help may be needed.

5. Acceptance: This follows when anger and depression have been worked through. It is the final acceptance of the loss. One never completely recovers from a significant experience of loss. There will always be certain emotional vulnerabilities remaining. It is as if we wear a coat with grief in many of the pockets for the remainder of our lives. But every pocket isn't filled with sorrow, and the coat should become a lot less heavy from unresolved grief the older it becomes. Eventually we will accept what has happened to us and see our sorrows as a part of our growth. It is only when we cannot accept suffering and sorrow as a part of our existence that we become traumatized by life.

According to Veninga, there is one marvelously redeeming motive for enter into one's sorrow. Once you have experienced the seriousness of your loss, you will be able to experience the wonder of being alive. It is a fact that once you experience pain, it in fact sensitizes you to joy.[8]

In the words of Abraham Maslow, "The confrontation with

death ... makes everything look so precious, so sacred, so beautiful that I feel more strongly than ever the impulse to live it, to embrace it, and to let myself be overwhelmed by it. My river has never looked so beautiful. . . . Death, and its ever present possibility, makes love, passionate love, more possible. I wonder if we could love passionately, if ecstasy would be possible at all, if we knew we'd never die."[9]

Healing comes with acceptance. Repeatedly, life propels us to release, surrender attachments, beliefs. To resist loss is ultimately to resist life. Life is and always has been in a constant state of turmoil. Loss weaves its way through the very fabric of life. We cannot fully say "yes" to life until we can say "yes" to death. It is difficult for us to accept the fact that life and loss come in the same package.

Characteristic 3: Those who survive a tragedy have learned to transcend their guilt.

Guilt can tear an individual's psychological support structure to shreds. In so doing, guilt delays recovery more than any other factor.[10] Let's face it, we all could have loved better many of the people close to us; our parents, our children, our spouses, our friends, our brothers and our sisters, even ourselves. We feel guilty at a time of loss because we are human beings. Because we are human we will always be capable of greater wisdom in our minds than in our deeds.

The hardest thing is learning certain things about ourselves that we don't especially want to know. Growing can be painful. It is not easy to acknowledge that we have made mistakes, wrong decisions and choices, and that some of our suffering may have been brought on by ourselves. When grief is progressing at its best we come face to face with ourselves in this way. It becomes clear what is important in life. We begin to see that many precious moments have been wasted.

As I mentioned earlier, there are different kinds of guilt. Neurotic guilt concerns things over which we have very little control. Or feeling guilty because we can't be perfect and have limitations because of our humanness. Existential guilt is another kind of guilt, and it is appropriate. It is the guilt we experience because we know that we have not fulfilled our potential. It is guilt over the fact that we have not used our talents and have wasted away our God-given gifts.

Going through a crisis can have the positive result of forcing us to face our existential guilt. This can have the effect of transforming our lives. I know that, for me, having faced some very dark moments in my own life made me much more aware of just how precious life is. Experiencing losses made me face my own vulnerability. That was a profound experience. I felt a strong need to make my life significant in some way. It made me want to create my own meaning in life because I now knew that no one could do that for me. Creating a personal meaning was a solitary responsibility.

By facing my own powerlessness in the face of certain realities of life, I began to realize just how much power I still possessed. It made me see how much personal responsibility I had to make my life count. In some ways I was powerless, but I did have the power to make certain things happen. I might be powerless and vulnerable but I also was potent and powerful too.

My losses resulted in my development of a new philosophy of life. I now knew that I had a sacred responsibility to make something of my life. I was given certain talents and abilities, and it was up to me to use these and constantly work at achieving my potential. I was facing my own existential guilt.

My experiences of loss gave me the opportunity to reexamine my life and make the necessary changes. I now knew how important it was for me to be able to come to the end of my life with a sense of integrity. I would have integrity if, on my deathbed, I could confront myself and acknowledge that my life did have a meaning. I would need to be able to face myself and know that I had fulfilled my mission to the best of my ability. If I could do that, then I believed that I would die in peace.

It became very important to me to not be at death's door

and have to reflect back on my life with a sense of existential disgust. I did not want to have to admit to myself that I had wasted my life and that I had not grown. That would be agonizing. I intended to make sure that such an experience didn't happen to me.

Transcending our guilt and making peace with ourselves is not easy. But those who survive a tragedy have discovered an important lesson: it does little good to punish ourselves. As Alexander Graham Bell once observed, "When one door closes, another opens, but we often look so long and so regretfully upon the closed door that we do not see the one that has opened for us."[11]

Characteristic 4: If you want to survive a crisis, you need a reason to live.

I do not believe that the negative experiences that happen to us in our lives have a meaning when they happen to us. And, as Rabbi Kushner so aptly states, there is really no good reason that would cause us to accept them willingly. But we can give them a meaning. We can redeem these tragedies from senselessness by imposing meaning on them. The question we should be asking is not, "Why did this happen to me? What did I do to deserve this?" That is really an unanswerable, pointless question. A better question would be: *"Now that this has happened to me, what am I going to do about it?"*[12]

Philosophers have long suggested that there exists within each of us a reservoir of hope. Within the essence of our being there is a real possibility that life can change for the better. We know that others facing equally troubling situations have been able to transcend their loss. This hope, this "expectancy of something more," seems to be at the heart of the recovery process. We need to believe that our loss will not have been in vain.[13]

What seems to demarcate those who survive a heartbreak from those who don't is a willingness to ask the poignant questions that relate to life and death, purpose and chaos. The answers may never be found, but by becoming a friend to the questions a small step toward inner healing is taken.[14]

When we lose a part of ourselves through illness, an accident, the loss of a loved one, the persons we are and have the potential to become must be resurrected in new form. As we learn from the loss of something of value, our loss is transformed. A situation that takes away something of value can also give us something new.

That is just how I felt about my program for displaced homemakers. I felt that if I could help other women in similar situations I would somehow transform my own loss. Who was better able to help these women than I who had also suffered such a loss? As difficult as my personal tragedy was, it could be of tremendous benefit in helping others. I would share with other women my personal story and thereby give them a role model. I was an example that each of us has the capacity to pick ourselves up and go on. We can survive, learn and grow.

My book *Mothers Are People Too* is another example of how I attempted to transform my own tragedy. I had lost custody of my three sons when I went through my divorce. It was at a time when men had just begun to fight women over custody and the courts were responding by giving custody of children to fathers. In a study conducted by Phyllis Chesler, and reported in her book *Mothers on Trial*, seventy percent of custodially challenged mothers lost custody. Now these were good mothers who had had the primary responsibility of child care during their marriages. The reason you do not hear more about mothers losing custody is because most men don't want custody of children. If they do, Chesler reports that seventy percent will succeed.[15] My ex-husband was one of those successes.

I wrote *Mothers Are People Too* as part of my own grief process during that painful time. I also hoped that what I had to say would be of help to other women. About a year later, my son, who was nineteen at the time, told me of an experience that still brings tears to my eyes.

He was talking to his female supervisor one day at his place of summer employment. She had had some personal problems and had lost custody of her children. She was really grieving over her loss. She mentioned to my son that her counselor had given her a book to read and that it had helped her immensely. She mentioned that she was sure that the author of the book must have gone through something similar because her comments were so true and pertinent. She told my son that the book was *Mothers Are People Too* by Anita Spencer.

What this lady did not realize was that she was talking to the son of the author; his last name is different than mine. But he piped up and said with a great deal of pride, "You don't know it, but that's my mom." I can't tell you just how moved I was when my son told me about this incident.

The fact that my writing had in some way helped that woman meant so much to me. The loss of my children had caused me a tremendous amount of sorrow, and I had hoped that my book would somehow transform my pain into something positive. I was especially moved by this story because my son was so proud of me. I could hear the pride in his voice. And having a significant influence on my children was something I had continually striven to achieve.

I just kept telling myself that I could be just as good a mother to my sons even though they were not with me every day. As devastated as I was when I lost custody, an inner part of me knew that no one could take my children from me. I vowed I would allow no one to have that kind of power. My son's story was a clear illustration to me that who I had become did have a significant impact on my children. I had again transformed my loss.

An important truth of life is that we each need a reason to live. We need to discover our own "meaning" as we discussed earlier in Chapter 3. It is important to make a commitment to life. It is this commitment that saves us and is well illustrated in the following story.

The Greeks had a legend about a man named Sisyphus who was banished by Zeus to a desert island, an island which had nothing on it to keep him occupied. And after a while Sisyphus started losing his mind. Then one day he took it into his head to push a big rock up the mountain on the island, and all day long he labored with the big rock, pushing it and pushing it in the hot sun, until at night, with the top of the hill almost in sight, he finally gave up and let the rock roll down the hill again. He did this again the next day, and the next, and for many months to come, and though he never reached the top of the mountain with his rock, when they finally found him he was sane, just as sane as he'd ever been.[16]

What is important in this story is that Sisyphus found a reason to live. We all must do that if we are to transcend a crisis. We need a reason to go on living. One way to do this is to make a commitment to something bigger than ourselves.

The Rewards of Surviving

There is no getting around the fact that our losses do change our lives dramatically. The unavoidable reality is that one can never be the same. Sometimes we are saddened by this fact and sometimes we are relieved. Maybe we didn't like the person we were in the past. I know that I have grown so much from my losses that I am hardly recognizable from that woman I was ten years ago. I really would not like to be that person that I was in the past. I am sorry certain losses have happened to me but I am not sorry that sorrow has changed me dramatically and that my life is much more fulfilling. I have gained too much that is too precious ever to go back again.

Life asks us eventually to transcend the grief, pain, rage, might-have-beens, regrets, dreams, and plans. And by that transcendence, we enlarge our compassion and our wisdom. According to Viktor Frankl, life is never lacking a meaning. We will understand this only if we recognize that there is a potential meaning to be found even beyond work and love. We must not forget that we may also find meaning in life even when confronted with a hopeless situation as its helpless victim, when facing a fate that cannot be changed. "For what then counts and matters is to bear witness to the uniquely human potential at its best, which is to transform a tragedy into a personal triumph, to turn one's predicament into a human achievement. When we are no longer able to change a situation—just think of an incurable disease, say, an inoperable cancer—we are challenged to change ourselves."[17]

Of course it is very difficult even to want to gain from our losses a life that is spiritually and emotionally richer than the life before. Especially in the beginning, we want to protect our grief and therefore we resist any attempt at growing or learning from it. It feels like a betrayal to gain something positive from our loss. The problem with that is that even if we wanted to remain the persons that we previously were, it simply is not possible. We either grow from a crisis or become damaged by it. But we cannot remain the same.

As I mentioned before, I would never want to go back to being the person I was earlier. I benefited so much from my pain. I now see how wise it was not to have wasted the opportunities that life was offering me during my times of crisis. To have done so would have been a real shame. I was in pain anyway, so why not derive some benefit from the experience. Each of us must find our own way to survive a crisis. We have the responsibility of discovering for ourselves how we can grow from an experience of suffering.

There is no more searching test of the human spirit than the way it behaves when fortune is adverse and it has to pass through a prolonged period of disappointing failures. Then comes the real proof of the man. Achievement, if a man has the ability, is a joy; but to take hard knocks and come up smiling, to have your mainsail blown away and then rig a sheet on the bowsprit and sail on—this is perhaps the deepest test of character (Harry Emerson Fosdick)[18]

Chapter 6

The Process of Healing

There is no getting around the fact that healing takes time and that there are always going to be scars. Loss is a lesson in vulnerability. It teaches us that we have no guarantee against having to give up the the people and things that are most precious to us. Most people, if they have not suffered any major losses, go boldly about the business of daily living, undaunted by an awareness of the catastrophes that could happen to them. But people who are grieving are not able to do that. They lose their sense of omnipotence and innocence and never fully regain it.

We never become fully desensitized to past pain in our lives. Just when we think we are over it, it comes back again. Even years later when a certain situation comes along that evokes the same emotional response, the pain will return. These are the scars of bitter grief. But these scars can be viewed positively. They are part of us and our struggle to develop our own unique personality. These scars are the reminder that we are indeed human.

Sometimes painful experiences make us want to retreat from life in order to protect ourselves from any future pain. I heartily agree with Rabbi Kushner when he tells us that we must remember that whenever we protect ourselves from loss by teaching ourselves not to care or not to let anyone get too close to us, we are really losing a part of our soul. We need to understand that part of being alive is to feel pain. If we hide from this fact we will become less alive.[1]

The danger is that if we believe that in order for life to be good we have to avoid pain, we may become so good at not feeling pain that we will learn not to feel anything at all. We won't feel joy, or love, or hope. We will become emotionally dead. We will then learn to live our whole lives within a narrow emotional range. Our lives will become monotonous. Because of our fear of pain, we will have mastered the art of detachment so well that nothing will be able to reach us emotionally.[2]

Healing is a slow process and allows no short cuts. You must allow yourself to fully grieve. Then slowly, gradually, renewal of the spirit begins. Joy reappears. Its like finding a small dim light at the end of a tunnel, and watching it grow brighter. The person begins to adjust to the loss and to gain confidence in new ways of functioning.

What is joy? My experience of joy is a *solid* feeling, a kind of affirmation of life that holds me up even in times of grief or despair. It is peace. Joy can be the result when proper healing has taken place. In order to heal properly, we must care for the *whole* of our beings—body, mind, spirit, and emotions.

First, we must get in touch with our body. If we are feeling bad emotionally, if we don't get proper food and rest and exercise, then our body will be damaged. This is a time to remember the philosophical truth of human existence that we are "embodied" and have the responsibility to care for our bodies. And one of the very important essentials to healing is to take good care of our bodies by getting the proper nourishment, rest and exercise.

Second, we must be aware of the needs of our mind. As we have discussed in earlier chapters, we must find meaning in in our daily lives. I found it very helpful to get involved in something bigger than myself, to be committed to something. I also found it helpful to stretch or challenge my mind. It may help to be with people who are intellectually stimulating. Some of my best creative thinking happens when I am around other people who are also in touch with their own creativity.

Third, we must strengthen the emotional part of our lives. We can do this by developing a good network of friends. It has been said that more good therapy is accomplished over a cup of coffee in someone's kitchen than on all of the psychiatrist's couches in the world. Having good friends to help you through some of the emotional trauma can be extremely helpful.

Fourth, we need to pay attention to our spiritual life. This can be in the form of incorporating daily meditation into our life or just reading some kind of timeless material—such as Shakespeare, Plato, Aristotle, the Bible, the Koran etc. It is very important that we do something for our spirit every day.

We must be the caretaker of our whole selves. We need to strive to maintain a balance between our body, mind, emotions, and spirit. Taking care of these four areas will do much for the healing process. And part of the healing is learning to accept that joy and sorrow go hand in hand.

Then a woman said, Speak to us of Joy and Sorrow.

And he answered:

Your joy is your sorrow unmasked.

And the selfsame well from which your laughter rises was
    oftentimes filled with your tears.

And how else can it be?

The deeper that sorrow carves into your being, the more
    joy you can contain.

Is not the cup that holds your wine the very cup that was
    burned in the potter's oven?

And is not the lute that soothes your spirit, the very wood
    that was hollowed with knives?

When you are joyous, look deep into your heart and you
    shall find it is only that which has given you sorrow
    that is giving you joy.

When you are sorrowful look again in your heart, and you
    shall see that in truth you are weeping for that which
    has been your delight.

Some of you say, "Joy is greater than sorrow," and other
    say, "Nay, sorrow is the greater."

But I say unto you, they are inseparable.

Together they come, and when one sits alone with you at

your board, remember that the other is asleep upon
your bed.
Verily you are suspended like scales between your sorrow
and your joy.
Only when you are empty are you at standstill and balanced.
When the treasure-keeper lifts you to weigh his gold and
his silver, needs must your joy or your sorrow rise or
fall (Kahlil Gibran).[3]

I always tell my patients that recovering from a crisis is like
recovering from open heart surgery. We must give ourselves a
great deal of tender, loving care. And just as we would give ourselves time to physically recover from surgery, we must give ourselves plenty of time to emotionally recover as well.

Most of us suffer from some degree of low self-esteem.
When people come to me after suffering a loss or a heartbreak,
I always prescribe that they spend time having what I call a "love
affair with themselves." Such an affair involves accepting themselves with all their strengths and weaknesses. It is so hard for
us to accept our limitations. We want so much to pretend that
we are not flawed. It is such a relief when we can finally love
and accept our blemished selves. This is the time to remember
the existential truth that the only unconditional love is the love
we have for ourselves. All other loves are conditional. To have a
love affair with ourselves is to come to appreciate our own inherent worth.

There is a Hasidic story about a very poor rabbi
named Rabbi Eizik, son of Yekel of Cracow, who dreamed
that someone bade him look for a treasure under a bridge
leading to the king's palace in Prague. When the dream
reappeared for the third time, Rabbi Eizik set out for
Prague. But the bridge was guarded day and night, and be
dared not arouse suspicion by digging so he waited, walking around the bridge from sunrise to sundown. Finally,

the captain of the guards asked if he could help him. Rabbi Eizik, seeing that he was a kindly man, told him about his dream and how he had come all this way from a distant country. The captain laughed. "So to please a dream you have worn out all that shoe leather and come all this way," he said to Rabbi Eizik. "If I had as much faith in my dreams as you have in yours, I would have gone to Cracow to look for treasure under the stove of a Jew named Rabbi Eizik, son of Yekel. Wouldn't I have been a fool?"

Rabbi Eizik thanked him for his trouble, bowed, traveled home, dug up the treasure under his stove, and built a house of worship with the money. So that every day he could thank God for helping him to understand his treasure was not in some distant place but in the place where he stood every day—which is to say wherever he himself was.[4]

Accepting ourselves with all our imperfections is not denying the responsibility we all have for improving ourselves. That would mean that we were refusing to grow. But it is the understanding that we all make mistakes and that these mistakes can help us to progress and achieve our potential. This is a time to remind ourselves again that the goal of personality development is "wholeness" and not "perfection."

Few people have the correct picture of what it means to individuate. Most of us still think that individuating means becoming a sort of superman who has absolute power over his instincts, who is entirely spiritualized, who loves everybody and whom everybody loves, selfless, always ready to help, always just and good, etc.—in a word, a person who has attained perfection. This is the Christian ideal imprinted on the West and held up to us in childhood as the goal of our character development.[5]

This is not what Jung had in mind and is not achievable. No wonder we all wound up feeling so terrible about ourselves. The individuation process does not aim at perfectionism, but only at helping a man to become in the truest sense what he in fact is, and not to hide behind the ideal mask which is so easily mistaken for his true essence. The endeavor to follow the rules and regulations of society in every way is a perfectionism that all too often leads not to perfection but to a neurosis instead.[6]

As I mentioned in Chapter 6 in the discussion of evil, human imperfection has clung to all of us ever since the expulsion from Paradise. Many people easily fall into the error of believing that perfection is attainable in principle here on earth, and forget that it is at most something to be aimed at. Though it can be approached, it can never be reached.

When you have a love affair with yourself you take these facts into account. You develop personal goals that are achievable and stop berating yourself for not being perfect. The truth is that we are *not* perfect: we are human, which means that we are afraid, limited, confused, mean, altruistic, generous, envious, sad, glad, energetic, tired, clear, understanding, angry, and many other things by turns and together. In this important context the word *together* alludes to accepting, as much as we can, all aspects of the humanity of ourselves. This means living as real, alive people participating in the real, here-and-now world.

If we can accept the limits of the human condition then we can begin to accept ourselves as a result. This raises our self esteem and promotes the healing process necessary for our recovery from a crisis. With healing comes acceptance. We begin to see that our crisis has had some value—that pain has its own intrinsic worth. We then start looking on pain in a different light.

> And a woman spoke, saying, Tell us of Pain.
> And he said:
> Your pain is the breaking of the shell that encloses your
>   understanding.
> Even as the stone of the fruit must break, that its heart may
>   stand in the sun, so must you know pain.
> And could you keep your heart in wonder at the daily mir-
>   acles of your life, your pain would not seem less won-
>   drous than your joy;

And you would accept the seasons of your heart, even as
   you have always accepted the seasons that pass over
   your fields.
And you would watch with serenity through the winters of
   your grief.
Much of your pain is self-chosen.
It is the bitter potion by which the physician within you
   heals your sick self.
Therefore trust the physician, and drink his remedy in si-
   lence and tranquillity:
For his hand, though heavy and hard, is guided by the
   tender hand of the Unseen,
And the cup he brings, though it burn your lips, has been
   fashioned of the clay which the Potter has moistened
   with His own sacred tears (Kahlil Gibran).[7]

As I mentioned in Chapter 5, one of the best ways to recover
from a crisis is to find a way to transcend it. What "grief work"
involves is finding a way to replace that which at first seems irre-
placeable. You can do this in a number of ways.

As I mentioned earlier, I began a program for displaced
homemakers, and used that as a way of resurrecting my loss.
After an initial grieving period, I set about finding something
positive to do with all my pain and anger. We have oftentimes
viewed anger as totally negative but it also has a very positive
aspect. There is a tremendous amount of energy released with
anger. And I was certainly angry! But I used that anger constructively by creating a program where I could help others in
similar situations. It did not take away my loss but it was a way
of redeeming my personal tragedy.

This is just one example of how to transcend a crisis. Many
other people who have had loved ones die of an incurable illness
have spent much energy in raising money for research or helping
other families deal with the same disease. I have seen parents
whose children have died in car accidents as a result of drunk
drivers spend countless hours in working toward tougher drunk

driving laws. There are numerous other examples. What all these people have done is to learn from their personal loss something of value that benefits themselves and others. In this way, they have transformed their loss.

One of the best examples of how to transcend a crisis is contained in the following story:

There is an old Chinese tale about the woman whose only son died. In her grief, she went to the holy man and said, "What prayers, what magical incantations do you have to bring my son back to life?" Instead of sending her away or reasoning with her, he said to her, "Fetch me a mustard seed from a home that has never known sorrow. We will use it to drive the sorrow out of your life." The woman set off at once in search of that magical mustard seed. She came first to a splendid mansion, knocked at the door, and said, "I am looking for a home that has never known sorrow. Is this such a place? It is very important to me." They told her, "You've certainly come to the wrong place," and began to describe all the tragic things that had recently befallen them. The woman said to herself, "Who is better able to help these poor unfortunate people than I, who have had misfortune of my own?" She stayed to comfort them, then went on in her search for a home that had never known sorrow. But wherever she turned, in hovels and in palaces, she found one tale after another of sadness and misfortune. Ultimately, she became so involved in ministering to other people's grief that she forgot about her quest for the magical mustard seed, never realizing that it had in fact driven the sorrow out of her life.[8]

This lady can be a real role model for all of us. Her ministry to others enabled her to heal in a way that benefited herself and others as well. There is no getting around the fact that healing is a process and that it takes time. The best ways that I have found to get through this process are to take good care of yourself, develop a more loving relationship with yourself, and find some way to transcend your grief.

What I think helped me the most in my healing process was to see my crisis as an opportunity to work on my development. By viewing it as being constructive, it put a different light on my pain. I began to see trouble as only opportunity in work clothes. I wasn't denying my pain. I certainly felt plenty of that. But I did develop a positive attitude toward it that made me stop being a victim. I used the anger that I felt about life's injustices as energy fuel to transform my life.

The spirit is capable of healing. It takes both time and effort. The end result of the healing process can be a changed life— a new life with more meaning, contentment, strength, courage and joy. "Stars may be seen from the bottom of a deep well, when they cannot be seen from the top of the mountain. So are many things learned in adversity, which the prosperous man dreams not of."[9]

Chapter 7

Putting It All Together— Growing Through a Crisis

We have explored a number of areas that are important in order to properly resolve a crisis and grow. If we are able to use the crises in our lives as catalysts for growth and change, we will have become like Prince Five-Weapons discussed in Chapter 1. We will no longer need to fear the "Sticky-Hair" ogres that periodically appear along life's way. We will have become strengthened by our experiences and learned from them that the winds of life may bend us, but that they cannot break us.

It may be helpful to summarize the major points that we have discussed and draw a road map that can be used as a guide when going through a crisis. Whether you are in a crisis now or have been in the past, this map should help give you a sense of direction.

As you will recall from earlier chapters, there are two types of crises. A Type I crisis is developmental in nature. This is the kind of crisis that is caused by anxiety that signals the need to make necessary changes in the direction or quality of your life. We grow by listening to this anxiety. A Type II crisis is the kind that is unexpected, accidental or situational. It is not expected. This crisis forces us to make some kind of change in our lives. We have to react to it. We have no choice. It also gives us an opportunity to work on developmental issues that we have ignored because the anxiety signaling a Type I crisis was previously ignored.

If you are one of those people who have never experienced

a Type II crisis, you have so far been fortunate. If you have never dealt with a Type I crisis, it is probably because you were not aware of what was occurring during times in your life when you were unhappy, anxious, or depressed. You did not realize that those feelings and emotions were trying to tell you that you needed to make some changes in your life. In other words, you were experiencing a Type I crisis and didn't even know it.

It is also possible that you have had either a Type I or Type II crisis in your life but were not able to successfully resolve it. The experience of a crisis may have frightened you to such an extent that you have become immobilized as a result. You may be too afraid to ever love again or try new experiences because you don't want to risk another failure. Or perhaps you have become bitter and depressed as a result of past occurrences. Another possibility is that you never worked through the grief and are now stuck in what is referred to as "prolonged grief." If any of the above are true, it is never too late to gain some invaluable insights from this past experience and use it now in order to grow.

A Map for Growth
The Stages and Tasks of a Crisis

The stages and tasks which I will describe do not necessarily occur in a linear fashion. One stage does not directly lead into the next. There will be some overlapping and some moving back and forth between stages. What I am outlining is a general direction. Growth does not occur in a smooth progression. There are always peaks and valleys—first we move forward and then we move backward. This is also true about progressing through a crisis. You just keep moving through it and trust in the process. If you are open and honest you will find your way through the maze. There is a will to survive and grow in all of us that can be called forth during times of distress. Just trust your own inner process and take the journey along with me.

Stage One
The Crisis Hits

If this is a Type II crisis, accidental or unexpected in nature, no one will have to tell you that you are in it. If it is developmental—Type I in nature—you will know that you are in it because of feelings of anxiety, unhappiness or depression. You may be asking yourself questions like "Is this all there is?" or "Why am I so unhappy?" If you do not know that feelings like these are a sign of a Type I crisis, you may ignore it by pushing the feelings away. The resulting problem is that the feelings don't go away and just keep mounting until the anxiety or depression is so severe that you are forced to deal with the crisis.

One of the problems with a Type I crisis is that you become confused because, unlike Type II crises that have a definite cause, these crises have no exact precipitating event. If no one has informed you about developmental crisis, you can become very distressed when you are unable to pinpoint an exact cause of your unhappiness. Hopefully, the previous chapters have given you some insight into the developmental and philosophical causes of Type I crises. Once you become aware that you are in a crisis state your first task is to become stabilized.

This stabilization process takes four to six weeks and progresses in a roller coaster fashion. It begins with every day being difficult. Then one day things seem a bit better. The next two or three days are bad again. You may then have two good days before another bad day occurs. Near the end of the six weeks, most days are survivable. When I say that some days are better than others I don't mean to suggest that any days are happy ones. The difference between a bad day and a good day is a matter of degree. A good day is one when things do not appear to be quite as bleak. It is a day that you think you may make it through to the next.

It is important to remember that recovery during this stage

does not progress with steady improvement. I have had many patients react with upset when they had a good day followed by a bad day. They thought they had regressed back to square one. I would reassure them that they were indeed improving even though bad days still occurred. By the end of six weeks the good days should outnumber the bad. Also, be aware of the fact that bad days will still occur on occasion even many months after a crisis hits.

Task 1
Stabilization—Taking Care of Physical Needs

This is the period of initial shock. Something unbelievable has happened. It hits you out of the blue (Type II) or you become so depressed or anxious that you are unable to function normally. You may not be sleeping or eating properly. It is extremely important to have a support system now. This could be a family member, a friend, or a trained professional. If you are in a situation where there is no one around during this time, call a hot line in your community or a local church. They will be able to put you in touch with support services that are available to you during a crisis. It is very important that someone be monitoring you during this stage because, depending on the level of shock or distress, you may not be able to adequately care for yourself.

Some people need medication to get them through this stage. Get in touch with your family physician, tell him or her what has happened, and seek expert advice. Sometimes people refuse to take any medications because they see that as being weak or are afraid that they will become addicted to medication. It is seldom the case that a person with no history of substance abuse becomes addicted to drugs during a time of crisis. The most important thing right now is that you take proper care of yourself. You may need medication to help you sleep or to reduce the severity of depression or anxiety. Remind yourself that the medication will only be needed temporarily until your condition has become stabilized.

Task 2
Stabilization—Taking Care of Emotional Needs

You need the support of family and friends. Just knowing that someone is standing by is important. In the beginning you may be too numb or shocked to cry. But after a week or two, your emotions will begin to come to the surface. As I mentioned in Chapter 4, no one can go through the grieving process for you. But you do need to know that others care and are there to support you. If you are feeling suicidal, it is imperative that you get professional help. There is a suicide and crisis hot line or an emergency mental health hot line in most cities. Do not hesitate to call them. They have been trained to help people in crisis situations and there is no charge for this service.

It is important that you do whatever is necessary to obtain emotional release. I described earlier what was helpful for me. I found crying to be extremely beneficial. Don't be afraid to cry. And don't be afraid to ask for help from those who are standing by. It can sometimes be very hard to ask for support but don't forget about that "giant bank account in the sky" mentioned in Chapter 5. It is there for you to withdraw from and you can deposit support later when you are feeling stronger.

Task 3
Stabilization—Taking Care of Psychological Needs

You will need to take certain steps to psychologically prepare yourself for change. You can do this by telling yourself that you are going to make it through this period. It helps some people to read inspirational literature. Hopefully, you have developed a philosophy of life that you can use to reassure yourself that what is happening will have some positive benefit.

During this first stage, it is very difficult to believe that anything positive could result from so much pain. You may very well react with anger if someone even mentions that you might grow from this experience. Don't worry, it's all right to be angry. It is very important that seeds start getting planted right now that a rebirth experience is going to occur. Keep reassuring yourself that things will get better and something positive will result even if you don't believe it right at this moment. What I am asking you to do is to fan the fires of "hope." I believe that it is crucial to do this during this first stage in order to survive and grow from this difficult experience.

It is also important to remind yourself that crises happen to everyone. This will help reduce self-blame or the belief that the crisis is a punishment for past wrongs. Also, the coping mechanisms that you may have successfully used in the past may not work now. This does not mean that you are a failure. Your helplessness should not be attributed to yourself or to the universe. It is a simple truth that anyone in your circumstances is going to be helpless because of factors outside of one's control. It is common to experience a great deal of helplessness during any crisis.

Stage Two
Gaining Some Insight

The first stage of becoming stabilized takes approximately four to six weeks. By the end of this first stage you are still in pain and distressed but you are able to eat and sleep more normally. Good days outnumber bad days and you begin to be more hopeful that you will survive. It is at this point that the second stage begins. If the first stage has lasted beyond six weeks, it is very important that professional help be sought. There are many community mental health clinics that have fees based on the ability to pay. Therefore, there is no reason to not get help.

As the second stage begins you may feel a sense of urgency to get on with life and for the crisis to be resolved. You may begin to feel desperate because you don't think that you can tolerate the situation much longer. You want a fast solution. Most crises (especially Type II) make you feel very out of control and powerless. I have yet to meet a normal person who enjoys feeling out of control. It is difficult to endure the anxiety that this entails. That is why most people want a quick resolution to a crisis.

Task 1
Coping by Developing Patience

It is important to remember that a quick resolution to a crisis is not always possible. And when it is possible, it may not be advisable. The desire to return to a state of relative equilibrium or emotional balance may result in a poor resolution of the crisis and a resultant failure to grow.

Learning to be patient is the first task at hand during this stage. This is the time to remember the old Chinese proverb: "The man who removes a mountain begins by carrying away small stones." You can not rush this second stage because now is the time where important insight can be gained. Self-examination and self-reflection take time.

All of us could use more experience in tolerating anxiety. Our society does not teach us how to do this very well. We live at a time when both pain and anxiety have received bad press. But if you have read the previous chapters you are probably beginning to realize the necessity of both. Society might as well be telling us that growing and changing is bad. Keep reminding yourself that anxiety is the catalyst for growth and that growth can not occur without it.

The experience of tolerating anxiety leads to the development of character. We develop emotional and psychological backbone. Practice makes perfect. This is a perfect opportunity to begin to do this if you never have done so before. Keep reminding yourself that no one can give this ability to you. It is something each of us must learn for ourselves.

Task 2
Taking a Developmental Inventory

In order to accurately do this task you must be honest with yourself. Self-honesty can be painful because it forces us to face our limitations. Just remember that to err is human. What is important is to learn from our mistakes. Hopefully, the previous chapters have made you more comfortable with your humanity and have shown you that the goal of life is not perfection but wholeness. If you are comfortable with that concept, self-reflection should prove to be much easier than in the past.

In order to take a psychological inventory you will need to review Erikson's "Stages of Man" discussed in Chapter 2. I will again list for you the various stages and the appropriate age that each conflict is initially addressed.

Stage	Developmental Task	Age
I	Trust vs. Mistrust	Infant to 1 year
II	Autonomy vs. Shame	1 to 3 years
III	Initiative vs. Guilt	3 to 6 years
IV	Industry vs. Inferiority	6 to 12 years
V	Identity vs. Role Confusion	adolescence
VI	Intimacy vs. Isolation	early adulthood
VII	Generativity vs. Stagnation	middle age
VIII	Integrity vs. Despair	maturity

After reviewing these stages and taking into account your own age, list the conflicts that you feel have been poorly resolved. I think that each of us is intuitively aware of our own weaknesses. All of these conflicts can certainly be reworked, but some may be more pressing than others depending on how successfully we have dealt with them in the past.

After you have listed these, prioritize them in order of importance. The first one on your list should be the one you feel has been least adequately worked through. (In my own case I would have listed as #1 "identity vs. role confusion.")

I would concentrate on the first three by listing some concrete ways you are going to work on them in the coming months. It is often helpful to have a friend or family member work on his or her own inventory at the same time. That way you will each be able to support one another. You might also consider joining a support group. Many communities have specific support groups in such categories as: the divorced, widows and widowers, cancer patients, parents of runaway teens, etc. You could work on this inventory together. I know that the women in my program for displaced homemakers found it very helpful to work together. They gave each other support and encouragement. It is oftentimes easier to take risks and make changes when others are doing the same. Courage becomes contagious.

Whether you do this inventory alone or with others, keep persevering. Give yourself a time line for accomplishing the tasks that you have listed. Begin with very simple goals such as reading a relevant book and reward yourself every time you complete a task. Gradually increase the difficulty level of the tasks. Start with simple tasks, because this better insures success. If you set goals that are too high, you only set yourself up for failure. Be patient with yourself.

Working on this psychological inventory is very rewarding. Each accomplishment becomes the breeding ground for the next accomplishment. Be creative in the way you address a conflict area. There are numerous ways to work on the "generativity vs. stagnation" issue. You could become involved in a worthy cause or do something concrete that would help make the world a better place. I often suggest to patients who wish to work on this particular area that they tell me what they consider to be the worst evil. I then have them do some small thing that would help eradicate or reduce the impact of that particular evil. There are many other possibilities. Use your imagination to help you grow.

You can keep working on your inventory forever. At different times in your life, you will find one area needing more work than at another time. You shift back and forth depending on what feels right intuitively. Growth is taking place throughout the life cycle and is never-ending. A crisis can be a reminder that we have much to do before we die. The pain and anxiety can be used to catapult us forward.

Task 3
Taking a Philosophical Inventory

In Chapter 3 we discussed what it means to be human. Perhaps you are much like me and have never given these issues much thought. I discovered that I had very unrealistic expectations about life. I was not prepared like Prince Five-Weapons for surviving in life. The young prince was confident in his training and hence fearless. He had been warned about the Ogre "Sticky-Hair" and was prepared to do battle. I had an inaccurate picture of the world and had never developed the skills necessary for battle. Just as the prince had completed military training, I needed to obtain a solid philosophical training in order to be adequately prepared for life.

What does it mean to be a person? What are the essential truths about human beings and the world around us? Prince Five-Weapons knew what was in the forest and entered prepared. I needed more knowledge of the forest before I could enter it prepared. The study of philosophy offers us the much needed insight into the truths of human existence.

Ask yourself which philosophical truth of human existence is being addressed in your particular crisis? Are you dealing with the issue of aloneness, or death, or meaning, or individual identity, etc.? Which issues stand out? Make a list of them. Go back and ask yourself what you know about that philosophical truth.

You may find it helpful to review the questions I posed after each truth. You may find it helpful to add some additional questions of your own.

The best way to do a philosophical inventory is to narrow down the truths to one or two that are the most important in your life right now. In clinical philosophy we believe that each truth must be understood, felt and integrated into our lives (referred to as the thought, feeling, action triad). Let me elaborate:

1. *The truth must be understood.* After you have identified the philosophical truth that is most relevant to your situation, ask yourself if you understand it thoroughly. If you do not, do some additional reading pertaining to that truth. Make sure that you have an intellectual grasp of the philosophical truth.

2. *The truth must be felt.* You are in an excellent position to do this if you are currently in a crisis state. Your feelings are now very raw and right on the surface. It is not enough to understand the concept of "aloneness." You must also know what it feels like to be all alone, to be totally abandoned. You must allow yourself to feel the pain and despair of this truth to the core of your being. Usually it is very hard to break through the thought-to-feeling barrier. This fact makes a crisis so very valuable. You have definitely broken through and are in tremendous pain. Significant growth can take place as a result.

3. *The truth must be integrated into your life.* You must express or manifest the thought and the feeling in a behavioral manner. How will your life be different because you have experienced this truth? Now that you recognize and have felt what it means to be alone, what changes will you make in your life? Your life must exhibit in some way the philosophical truth that you are focusing on. If your life is lacking in meaning and you both understand and have felt the experience of lack of meaning to the core of your being, what evidence are you giving the world that you have found meaning?

We need to go through this process with all the philosophical truths at some time in our life. To the degree these truths are integrated into our lives, we will be fulfilled. If they are not integrated, we will continue to experience symptoms in the form of depression, anxiety, guilt or even physical pain.

It is the premise of clinical philosophy that these existential truths must first be integrated into our lives before we work on the transpersonal or religious issues. Not that we can't be spiritual at the same time. It is just that we must not use the joy and peace of the spiritual world to deny the reality of this world. It is our destiny to be, to die. If we allow ourselves to focus on the issue of our immortality (a spiritual truth) we may use this as an excuse to not take our present life seriously. We may fool ourselves into thinking that we have all the time in the world. It is our destiny to fulfill ourselves and to develop our potential in this life regardless of our immortality.

Another way of looking at this is to say that we are born into this world with a sickness—philosophical ignorance. As we deal with the existential truths and integrate them into our lives, we become healthy. We then can move on to the spiritual and transpersonal truths and achieve "Superhealth." In other words, the soul moves from the decision for health to the decision for greatness. The soul's pilgrimage occurs in three stages: its illness, its health, and its holiness. The individual starts out with psychopathology, becomes healthy, and then is capable of moving on to self-actualization.[1]

Stage Three
Integration

Stage Two can take as long as necessary until the needed insight and growth is obtained. Stage Three begins at the time the integration of this new growth takes place. This integration is the result of a "rebirth experience" that occurred during Stage One and Stage Two. You will know you are in Stage Three when other people start commenting that you have changed. They may say things like "What's happened to you? You are like a different person?" Of course, the answer is that you are the same person but that you have changed dramatically as a result of growing.

A crisis can be a "death to resurrection" experience if you let it. But it takes a great deal of work as well as courage to be "reborn." When you have made it through to Stage Three you have been reborn.

Task 1
Continuing Your Growth

The integration of what you have learned from your crisis begins gradually. As you gain more insight into what has happened and make changes in your life as a result, more and more integration takes place. This is a time to be open to new experiences. You will be surprised at what begins to happen. All sorts of new opportunities and new people begin to enter your life. This is a very challenging and fulfilling time because you begin to see the limitlessness of your possibilities. You now have as your task the responsibility to continue to grow.

Task 2
Becoming a Role Model

It is very important that you share what you have learned with others. By so doing, you will also be giving yourself another opportunity to work on the developmental conflict of generativity vs. stagnation. You can do this in a number of ways. What is important is that other people learn how to grow from a crisis.

One way you can do this is to share your insights with others who are going through a crisis that is similar to the one that you have experienced. People will intuitively sense the truth of what you are sharing and will therefore learn a great deal from your example. They need to see the living proof that you have indeed survived a very negative experience and grown. It is so very important that people know that something negative can bring forth something extremely positive as aptly illustrated in this ancient parable.

> Each day the king sat in state hearing petitions and dispensing justice. Each day a holy man, dressed in the robe of an ascetic beggar, approached the king and without a word offered him a piece of very ripe fruit. Each day the king accepted the "present" from the beggar and without a thought handed it to his treasurer who stood behind the throne. Each day the beggar, again without a word, withdrew and vanished into the crowd.
>
> Year after year this precise same ritual occurred every day the king sat in office. Then one day, some ten years after the holy man first appeared, something different happened. A tame monkey, having escaped from the women's apartments in the inner palace, came bounding into the hall and leaped up onto the arm of the king's throne. The ascetic beggar had just presented the king with his usual gift of fruit, but this time, instead of passing it on to his treasurer as was his usual custom, the king handed it over to the monkey. When the animal bit into it, a precious jewel dropped out and fell to the floor.
>
> The king was amazed and quickly turned to his treasurer behind him. "What has become of all the others?" he asked. But the treasurer had no answer. Over all the years he had simply thrown the unimpressive "gifts" through a small upper window in the treasure house, not even bothering to unlock the door. So he excused himself and ran quickly to the vault. He opened it and hurried to the area beneath the little window. There, on the floor, lay a mass of rotten fruit in various stages of decay. But amidst this garbage of many years lay a heap of precious gems.[2]

This parable certainly illustrates in a dramatic way the fact that things are not always what they appear to be. And that which appears to be or is believed to be negative or undesirable may in fact be quite the opposite. Most people view a crisis as did the king. They see it as undesirable and want to get rid of it as soon as possible. They keep throwing away negative experiences and fail to see them as the gifts they are meant to be.

If you have gotten to Stage Three, you have recognized the ripe fruit that life presented you as a disguised gift. You have used it to grow. Your task now is to be like the monkey—to show others that a negative experience can be a very valuable gift. By so doing, you will have exemplified by your changed life that this precious gift is available to them as well.

Chapter 8

•

Crisis—A Pathway to Self-Actualization

Throughout this book we have discussed how a crisis can be a catalyst for growth and change. We have developed a process whereby we can gain insight from a very negative experience and use that insight in a positive way. The end result from all of this growth is to become whole and individuated. My favorite way of conceptualizing our task in life is to see it as self-actualization.

This subject of self-actualization has been an interest of mine for a long time. Because I am the kind of person who likes to know where I am headed, I do better when I have a clear destination in mind. As I studied psychology and philosophy, I came across this theory. It made a great deal of sense and seemed to be a very worthy goal.

The theory of self-actualization has become increasingly popular in modern psychological literature. The major proponent of this theory, Abraham Maslow, contends that a person becomes fully human only when his or her innermost nature is nurtured and developed to its fullest extent. Healthy people are those who have sufficiently gratified their basic needs for safety, belonging, love, respect and self-esteem so that they are motivated by trends to self-actualize. Their task then becomes to actualize as many of their potentials as possible.

Growth is defined by Maslow as the various processes which bring the person toward ultimate self-actualization. This process is going on throughout the life cycle. Growth involves the progressive gratification of basic needs to the point where they "disappear." It also involves motivations over and above these basic needs such as the development of talents, capacities, creative tendencies, constitutional potentialities, etc.[1]

Maslow asserts that there is present within the human being a tendency toward, or a need for, growing in a direction that can be summarized in general as self-actualization or psychological health. The individual has within a pressure toward unity of personality, toward spontaneous expressiveness, toward full individuality and identity, toward seeing the truth rather than being blind, and toward being creative.[2]

Among the objectively describable and measurable characteristics of the healthy human specimen are:

1. Clearer, more efficient perception of reality.
2. More openness to experience.
3. Increased integration, wholeness, and unity of the person.
4. Increased spontaneity, expressiveness; full functioning; aliveness.
5. A real Self; a firm identity; autonomy, uniqueness.
6. Increased objectivity, detachment, transcendence of Self.
7. Recovery of creativeness.
8. Ability to fuse concreteness and abstractness.
9. Democratic character structure.
10. Ability to love.

Healthy, self-actualized people are more integrated than the average person. They lack the fear of their own insides, of their own impulses, emotions, thoughts. They are more self-accepting than the average. This approval and acceptance of their deeper selves then makes it more possible to perceive bravely the real nature of the world and also makes their behavior more spontaneous (less controlled, less inhibited, less planned). They are less afraid of their own thoughts. They are less afraid of others' laughter or disapproval. They can let themselves be flooded by their emotions. In contrast, average and neurotic people wall off fear. They control, then inhibit, they repress, and they suppress. They disapprove of their deeper selves and expect others do too. Self-actualized people are more self-accepting due to their greater wholeness and integration.[4]

In the process of self-actualization, the person becomes less influenced by the deficiency problems of youth, and from the neurotic (or infantile, or "unreal") problems of life, and is able to face, endure and grapple with the "real" problems of life (the intrinsically and ultimately human problems, the unavoidable, the "existential" problems to which there is no solution). Problems don't disappear but there is a movement from transitional or unreal problems to real problems.[5]

As I thought about all of this and how crises influence our lives, it began to dawn on me that the growth-enhancing experiences of a crisis may well be what leads to self-actualization. People that we would define as highly self-actualized have undoubtably encountered a number of crises in their lives that have led to their high state of development.

It is also interesting to note that those characteristics of of a healthy, self-actualized human that Maslow has described are almost identical to what Carl Jung has described as a fully individuated person and to what the Existentialists would describe as an authentic human being. It is also clear that a self-actualized person has adequately resolved the eight stages of development proposed by Erikson. Therefore, a person who is growing throughout the life cycle and allowing Type I or Type II crises to be an impetus for change and growth is becoming self-actualized in the process.

When this thought dawned on me, I became very excited. It all began to make sense. I could see a plan. The world was not as nearly unpredictable or as out of control as I had thought. Once this realization hit, I began to relax and became much more accepting of life. I then began to wonder what it was that makes one person want to grow and find the answers to life while another person chooses to remain ignorant. My research into this

question gave me some answers that I would like to share with
you.

The Choice for Growth

All human beings have two sets of forces within them. One
set clings to safety and defensiveness out of fear, tending to re-
gress backward, hanging on to the past, afraid to grow away
from the primitive communication with the mother's uterus and
breast, afraid to take chances, afraid to jeopardize what they already have, afraid of independence, freedom and separateness.
Such fears as these were discussed previously.

The other set of forces impels them forward toward wholeness of Self and uniqueness of Self, toward full functioning of all
their capacities, toward confidence in the face of the external
world at the same time that they can accept their deepest, real,
unconscious Self.[6]

Therefore we can consider the process of healthy growth to
be a never-ending series of free choice situations, confronting all
individuals at every point throughout their lives, in which they
must choose between the delights of safety and growth, dependence and independence, regression and progression, immaturity
and maturity. Safety has both anxieties and delights; growth has
both anxieties and delights. We grow forward when the delights
of growth and anxieties of safety are greater than the anxieties
of growth and the delights of safety.[7]

What excites me is the fact that a crisis situation puts you
in circumstances where safety is no longer possible. This very fact
can become a motivation to grow because you really have nothing to lose. Safety is no longer there. This is precisely why I see
a crisis as such a tremendous opportunity.

Another important factor to consider is that assured safety
permits higher needs and impulses to emerge and grow toward
mastery. What this means is that if the choice is between giving
up safety or giving up growth, safety will ordinarily win out.

Safety needs are prepotent over growth needs. But when an individual is in a crisis (especially Type II), retreating back to safety is often just not possible. As a result, the individual may be propelled toward growth even in the absence of safety.

The Choice for Non-Growth

The above answers made a great deal of sense but I still wanted to know what causes some people to refuse to learn from life and grow. I believed that if I could discover the answer I might be able to discover a way to help those people when they came to me in distress. Why is it that so few people achieve the goal of self-actualization? Anybody *could* become a healthy person. Why doesn't everyone achieve this? My research gave me some additional answers.

We know already that the main prerequisite of healthy growth is gratification of the basic needs. But we have also discovered that unbridled indulgence and gratification has its own dangerous consequences. People can become narcissistic or develop "oral" personalities. They can become irresponsible, unable to bear stress, spoiled, immature, etc. There is now a large store of clinical and educational experience which allows us to make a reasonable guess that young children need not only gratification; they also need to learn the limitations that the physical world puts upon their gratifications, and they have to learn that other people seek for gratifications, too, even their mother and their father, e.g., their parents are not merely means to their ends. (This is the same as Philosophical Truth 10—The Other and the Reality Principle.)

What this means is that children must learn to control, delay and limit their demands. They must develop frustration-tolerance and learn self-discipline. It is only to the self-disciplined and responsible person that we can say, "Do as you will, and it will probably be all right."[8]

What other things stand in the way of growth? Why do so

many people have no real identity or power to make their own decisions and choices? Maslow gives the following reasons for nongrowth:

1. The impulses and directional tendencies toward self-ful-fillment, though instinctive, are very weak. In contrast with all other animals who have strong instincts, these impulses are very easily drowned out by habit, by wrong cultural attitudes toward them, by traumatic episodes, etc. Therefore, the problem of choice and of responsibility is far, far more acute in humans than in any other species.

2. There has been a tendency in western culture to assume that these instinctual needs of human beings, our so-called animal nature, are bad or evil. As a result of this, many cultural institutions are set up for the express purpose of controlling, inhibiting, suppressing and repressing this original human nature. But there can be no growth without access to this side of us.

3. There are two sets of forces pulling at the individual. In addition to the pressures forward toward health, there are also fearful-regressive pressures backward, toward sickness and weakness.[9]

Another answer to the question of why people fail to grow is given by Scott Peck. He believes that people's will to grow is nurtured not only by the love of their parents during childhood but also throughout their lives by grace, or God's love. He believes that it is because of grace that it is possible for people to transcend the trauma of loveless parenting. Grace is available to all people. All are cloaked in the love of God, but most choose not to heed the call of grace and reject its assistance. The reason is laziness, the original sin of entropy, with which all people have been cursed. Grace is the ultimate source of the force that pushes a person to evolve. It is entropy (laziness) that causes a person to resist that force. It takes self-discipline in order to grow.[10]

Peck looks on laziness as "original sin." He states: "Some of us may be less lazy than others, but we are all lazy to some extent. No matter how energetic, ambitious or even wise we may be, if we truly look at ourselves we will find laziness lurking at some level. It is the force of entropy within us, pushing us down and holding us all back from our spiritual evolution."[11]

A major form that laziness takes is fear—fear of change. I would agree with both Peck and Maslow that this is the reason many people drop out of psychotherapy. They come in because they are unhappy. They often hope to get a pill and all will be well. When they discover that becoming a happier person will involve work, they often become disillusioned. The therapist can support, encourage and give insight, but it is they who have to do the work. There is great resistance to changing. We would rather remain miserable then exert the effort necessary in order to change our dissatisfying lives.

Maybe I am just an optimist, but I really believe that people can find the courage to change. My experience as a therapist has shown me that it is the individuals who are going through a major crisis who are the most motivated to change. They know they need to do something. It is the crisis state that has caused them to seek help. These are precisely the people therapists can help the most due to the fact that the crisis state, by its very nature, is so conducive to change.

Another aspect that we must consider is the fact that we can never really understand human weakness without also understanding the basic human tendency toward health. Furthermore, we can never fully understand or help human strength without also understanding its weaknesses. If we wish to become more fully human, we must realize not only that we try to realize ourselves, but that we are often reluctant, afraid or unable to do so. Only by appreciating this dialectic between sickness and health can we help to tip the balance in favor of health.[12] Due to the circumstances and characteristics of a crisis, a person is in a better position to tip the balance in favor of health.

As I have mentioned in other chapters, growth has not only rewards and pleasures, but also many intrinsic pains. Each step forward is a step into the unfamiliar and is possibly dangerous.

It also means giving up something familiar, good and satisfying. It frequently means a parting and a separation, even a kind of death prior to rebirth, with consequent nostalgia, fear, loneliness and mourning. It also often means giving up a simpler and easier life in exchange for a more demanding, more responsible life. Growth forward happens in spite of these losses and therefore requires courage, will, choice, and strength.

It is especially true in the case of Type II crises that you cannot retreat to an easier and simpler life. That choice has been taken from you. This lack of choice can propel you in the direction of growth and change.

I would agree with Maslow that self-actualization does not mean a transcendence of all human problems. Conflict, anxiety, frustration, sadness, hurt and guilt can be found in healthy human beings. In general, the movement, with increasing maturity, is from neurotic pseudo-problems to the real, unavoidable, existential problems, inherent in human nature (even at its best). To be untroubled when one should be troubled can be a sign of sickness.[13] Sometimes it takes a crisis for smug people to be scared "into their wits."

The choice to not grow is certainly possible. All the evidence indicates that it is reasonable to assume that in practically every human being, and certainly in almost every newborn baby, there is an active will toward health, an impulse toward growth or toward the actualization of human potentialities. But we are also confronted with the very saddening realization that so few people make it. In reality, only a small proportion of the human population gets to the point of identity, selfhood, full humanness, or self-actualization. This happens even in a society like ours which is one of the most fortunate on the face of the earth. This is our great paradox. We need to understand "why" if we wish our society to achieve higher levels of development. The essential problem of human nature is the appreciation of its high possibilities, and simultaneously a deep disappointment that these possibilities are so infrequently actualized.

I have always been a visionary, one who always asks the bigger questions in life in the hopes of learning the answers and discovering new possibilities. Why, then, if we have this impulse to improve ourselves, to actualize our potentialities, do we often fail to do so? Besides the reasons that I have mentioned above and in previous chapters, what other reasons for nongrowth can there possibly be?

The Jonah Complex

Abraham Maslow has coined the phrase "the Jonah Complex." The "Jonah Complex" is the "fear of one's own greatness" or the "evasion of one's destiny" or the "running away from one's own best talents." In other words, it is certainly possible for most of us to be greater than we are in actuality. We all have unused potentialities or not fully developed ones. So often we run away from the responsibilities dictated (or rather suggested) by nature, by fate, even sometimes by accident, just as Jonah tried—in vain—to run away from his fate. This is similar to what Scott Peck referred to as the "original sin" of laziness.

The human condition causes us to fear our highest possibilities (as well as our lowest ones). We are generally afraid to become that which we can glimpse in our most perfect moments, under the most perfect conditions, under conditions of greatest courage. We enjoy and even thrill to the godlike possibilities we see in ourselves in such peak moments. And yet we simultaneously shiver with weakness, awe, and fear before these very same possibilities.[14]

Maslow further states that not only are we ambivalent about our own highest possibilities, we are also in a perpetual and universal conflict and ambivalence over these same highest possibilities in other people, and in human nature in general. This is due to the fact that the greatest people, simply by their presence and by being what they are, make us feel aware of our lesser worth, whether or not they intend to do so.[15]

Another reason we may fail to grow is due to our fear of being guilty of "sinful pride." For some people this evasion of one's own growth, setting low levels of aspiration, the fear of doing what one is capable of doing, and mock-humility are in fact defenses against grandiosity, arrogance or sinful pride. In order to invent or create, you must have the "arrogance of creativeness." But if you have the arrogance without the humility you become conceited. Therefore, you must be aware not only of the godlike possibilities within, but also of your existential limitations. You must be able to laugh at yourself and all your human pretensions. Maslow suggests that if you can be amused by the worm trying to be a god, then in fact you may be able to go on trying and being arrogant without fearing that you will become conceited or bring down upon yourself some evil curse. If you can laugh at yourself and use such a technique, you won't have to worry about "sinful pride."[16] What you will have then successfully done is to have made friends with your "shadow."

It is also true that we need truth and love it and seek it. And yet it is just as easy to demonstrate that we are also simultaneously *afraid* to know the truth. This is because certain truths carry automatic responsibilities which may be anxiety-producing. One way to evade the responsibility and the accompanying anxiety is simply to evade consciousness of the truth.[17]

We all have these higher needs and, at the same time, we have constructed defenses against these higher impulses. We have a love of beauty and an uneasiness with it. We have a love of good people and an irritation with them. We may search for excellence and yet tend to destroy it. These counter-values are stronger in neurotic people, but Maslow believes that we all must make our peace with these mean impulses within ourselves. The best way to do this is to change envy, jealousy, and nastiness into humble admiration, gratitude, appreciation, and adoration. This is the road to feeling small and weak and unworthy and *accepting* these feelings instead of needing to protect a spuriously high self-esteem by striking out. If we can do this, it will help resolve the "Jonah Complex."

Meeting the Challenge

The choice for growth is possible in spite of fear, laziness, apathy, and the "Jonah Complex." We can learn from life and we can move forward despite numerous obstacles. One of my favorite examples of a person who chose to grow even though he was confronted with numerous defeats is Abraham Lincoln. No matter what blows life dealt him he continued on, to become all that he could be. Just listen to the obstacles he had to overcome.

He lost his job in 1832.
He was defeated for the legislature, also in 1832.
He failed in business in 1833.
He was elected to the legislature in 1834.
He suffered the loss of his sweetheart, who died in 1835.
He suffered a nervous breakdown in 1836.
He was defeated for speaker of the state legislature in 1838.
He was defeated for nomination for Congress in 1843.
He was elected to Congress in 1846.
He lost his renomination for Congress in 1848.
He was rejected for the position of land officer in 1849.
He was defeated for the Senate in 1854.
He was defeated for the nomination for Vice-President of the United States in 1856.
He was defeated again for the Senate in 1858.[18]

In 1860, Abraham Lincoln was elected President of the United States. Who knows what this man would have accomplished if his life had not ended prematurely. He is such an example of the "will to grow." I am sure he would have achieved a high degree of self-actualization had he lived a full life-span.

I love to tell this story when I speak to groups of people because it generates hope. All of us need to be inspired to achieve our highest potential. As I mentioned earlier, self-actualization is a concept that has always intrigued me. Perhaps that was because I saw it as one of life's greatest challenges. Lincoln is a prime example of this. His life is another reminder of just how important a part crises can play in that process. I used to view pain in such a negative light that I was unable to see its possibilities.

I can now better understand the principle of duality or polarity, the fact that something can be very negative and positive at the same time. A crisis is very painful. There is no getting around this fact. But a crisis can be positive as well. It can provide us with an opportunity to grow and self-actualize. Such a state is never a final product. It is a process. If we are able to view it in this way, we will be able to see how any crisis can be a pathway to self actualization.

> I do not know what we are here for upon this wonderful and beautiful earth, this incalculably interesting earth, unless it is to crowd into a few short years every possible fine experience and adventure; unless it is to live our lives to the uttermost; unless it is to seize upon every fresh impression, develop every latent capacity; unless it is to grow as much as ever we have it in our power to grow (David Grayson).[19]

Conclusion

I have thought long and hard about the subject of pain and crisis. Because it frightened me so much as a child, I needed to find some way to understand its purpose. I now believe that I have found my answer. Perhaps M. Scott Peck, in his book *The Road Less Traveled*, put it best when he said: "Life is difficult." And the sooner we recognize the truth of this fact, the sooner we will be able to transcend it. Once we truly understand and accept the fact that life is difficult, really know this in the core of our being, the fact that life is difficult no longer matters. Once we can accept suffering as a part of life, it ceases in a sense to be suffering.[1]

Losses, failures and crises are an inevitable part of life. We need to begin to appreciate these experiences and their value. It is the premise of clinical philosophy that we should view our lives as having been merely a necessary apprenticeship. Perhaps it is only through our particular life that we were able to learn what we needed to know as a fulfilled person. The really crucial problem is that sometimes we refuse to hear the message that a particular crisis is trying to give us and the same problems keep repeating themselves over and over again. Consequently, it becomes imperative that we begin seeing crises in the same light as did the ancient Chinese—as opportunities riding on dangerous winds.

Now that I am an adult woman, I have a better understanding of God. I no longer pray to him for a trouble-free life. My prayers have since changed and are no longer those of a naive child. I now understand what Rabbi Kushner states so aptly:

We can pray to God for comfort and courage. We can't pray that He will make our lives free of problems; this won't happen, and it is probably just as well. People who pray for miracles usually don't get miracles.... But people who pray for courage, for strength to bear the unbearable, for the grace to remember what they have left instead of what they have lost, very often find their prayers answered. They discover that they have more strength, more courage than they ever knew themselves to have. Where did they get it? Perhaps their prayers helped them tap hidden reserves of faith and courage which were not available to them before.[2]

My experiences of crises have helped me develop a more mature understanding of God. Even in my darkest moments I did not blame God for my problems. I just came to accept that pain was a part of life and very necessary for my growth. As a crisis survivor and as one of the "walking wounded," I now trust in God's infinite wisdom and understand what truly loving him is all about.

We do not love God because He is perfect. We do not love Him because He protects us from all harm and keeps evil things from happening to us. We do not love Him because we are afraid of Him, or because He will hurt us if we turn our back on Him. We love Him because He is God, because He is the author of all the beauty and order around us, the source of our strength and the hope and courage within us, and of other people's strength and hope and courage with which we are helped in our time of need. We love Him because He is the best part of ourselves and of our world. That is what it means to love. Love is not the admiration of perfection, but the acceptance of an imperfect person with all his imperfections, because loving and accepting him makes us better and stronger.

Man depends on God for all things; God depends on

man for one. Without Man's love, God does not exist as God, only as creator, and love is the one thing no one, not even God Himself, can command. It is a free gift, or it is nothing. And it is most itself, most free, when it is offered in spite of suffering, of injustice, and of death.[3]

Notes

Introduction
1. Judith Viorst, *Necessary Losses* (New York: Simon and Shuster, 1986), pp. 15–16.
2. Charles L. Wallis, *Words of Life* (San Francisco: Harper & Row, 1966), p. 179.
3. Jo Petty, *Apples of Gold* (Norwalk, Connecticut: C. R. Gibson Co.), p. 20.
4. Ibid., p. 73.

Chapter 1
1. Gerald Caplan, *An Approach to Community Mental Health* (New York: Grune and Stratton, 1961), p. 18.
2. Jolande Jacobi, *The Way of Individuation* (New York: New American Library, 1965), p. 133
3. Ibid.
4. Ibid.
5. Ibid., p. 115.
6. Ibid., p. 116.
7. Merle Shain, *Hearts That We Broke Long Ago* (New York: Bantam Books, 1983), pp. 22–23.
8. Robert Veninga, *A Gift of Hope* (Boston: Little, Brown and Company, 1985), pp. 43–54.
9. Gail Sheehy, *Pathfinders* (New York: William Morrow and Co. Inc., 1981), p. 2.

Chapter 2
1. Viktor Frankl, *Man's Search for Meaning* (New York: Washington Square Press, 1963), p. 28.

2. Erik Erikson, *Childhood and Society* (New York: Norton & Co., 1963), p. 121.
3. Ibid., pp. 247–274.
4. Sheehy, p. 77.
5. Erikson, p. 254.
6. Shain, p. 34.
7. Peter Koestenbaum, *The Existential Crisis* (Campbell, Cal.: Institute for Clinical Philosophy, 1980), p. 68.
8. Sheehy, p. 86
9. Erik Erikson, *Identity: Youth and Crisis* (New York: Norton and Co., 1968), p. 124.
10. Sheehy, p. 90.
11. Sheehy, pp. 90–91.
12. Merle Shain, *When Lovers Are Friends* (New York: J. B. Lippincott Co., 1978), pp. 64–65.
13. Ibid., p. 65.
14. Erikson, 1963, p. 261.
15. Group for the Advancement of Psychiatry (GAP), *The Educated Woman* (New York: Charles Scribners & Sons, 1975), p. 149.
16. Erikson, 1963, p. 263–64.
17. Erikson, 1968, p. 136.
18. Shain, 1983, p. 71.
19. George R. Bach and Ronald M. Deutsch, *Pairing* (New York: Wyden, Inc., 1970), p. 223.
20. Kahlil Gibran, *The Prophet* (New York: Alfred A. Knopf, 1985), pp. 15–16.
21. Erikson, 1963, p. 267.
22. Viktor E. Frankl, *The Unheard Cry for Meaning* (New York: Simon & Schuster, 1978), p. 110.
23. Frankl, 1978, p. 106.
24. Peter Koestenbaum, *The Will to Freedom* (Campbell, Cal.: Institute for Clinical Philosophy, 1981), pp. 30–31
25. Peter Koestenbaum, *New Image of a Person* (Westport, Conn.: Greenwood Press, 1978), p. 357.

26. Erikson, 1963, pp. 268–69.
27. Erikson, 1968, pp. 139–141.
28. Harold. S. Kushner, *When All You've Ever Wanted Isn't Enough* (New York: Summit Books, 1986), p. 135.
29. Quoted in Jacobi, p. 16.
30. Veninga, pp. 210–11.

Chapter 3
1. Koestenbaum, 1980, p. 4.
2. Ibid.
3. Ibid., p. 5.
4. Ibid., p. 11.
5. Ibid., p. 12.
6. Ibid., p. 41.
7. Ibid., p. 9.
8. Ibid., p. 17.
9. Ibid., p. 12
10. Ibid., p. 41.
11. Ibid., pp. 43–51.
12. Shain, 1983, p. 12.
13. Kushner, p. 43.
14. Ibid., pp. 52–66.
15. Ibid., p. 67.
16. Koestenbaum, 1978, p. 231.
17. Koestenbaum, 1980, p. 75.
18. Shain, 1978, p. 38.
19. Ibid., p. 141.
20. Ibid., p. 73.
21. Ibid., p. 78.
22. Ibid., p. 80.
23. Ibid., pp. 80–93.
24. Shain, 1983, p. 68.
25. Koestenbaum, 1980, p. 95.
26. Wallis, p. 121.

27. Koestenbaum, 1980, p. 117.
28. Wallis, p. 91.

Chapter 4
1. Anne. M. Lindbergh, *Hour of Gold, Hour of Lead* (New York: McGraw-Hill, 1971), p. 215.
2. Shain, 1983, p. 21.
3. Kushner, p. 126.
4. Jacobi, p. 16
5. Ibid., p. 17.
6. Kushner, p. 99
7. Ibid.
8. John A. Sanford, *Evil: The Shadow Side of Reality* (New York: Crossroad, 1984), p. 40.
9. William Miller, *Make Friends with Your Shadow* (Minneapolis: Augsburg Publishing, 1981), p. 12
10. Ibid., p. 29.
11. Shain, 1978, p. 41.
12. Miller, p. 24.
13. Jacobi, p. 119.
14. Sanford, p. 40.
15. Jacobi, p. 120–21.
16. Ibid., p. 127.
17. Ibid., p. 131.
18. Ibid.
19. Denis Waitley, *The Seeds of Greatness* (New Jersey: Fleming H. Revel Co., 1983), pp. 67–68.
20. Miller, p. 71.
21. Ibid., p. 135.
22. Ibid., p. 12.
23. Shain, 1983, p. 78.

Chapter 5
1. Sheehy, p. 11.
2. Ibid., pp. 12–15.

3. Ibid., p. 89.
4. Veninga, p. 60.
5. Shain, 1978, p. 74.
6. Veninga, p. 70.
7. E. Kübler-Ross, *On Death and Dying* (New York: Macmillan & Co., 1969).
8. Veninga, p. 71.
9. Ibid., p. 277.
10. Ibid., p. 72.
11. Ibid., p. 77.
12. Harold S. Kushner, *When Bad Things Happen to Good People* (New York: Schocken Books, 1981), p. 136.
13. Veninga, p. 77.
14. Ibid., p. 211.
15. Phyllis Chesler, *Mothers on Trial* (New York: Mc Graw-Hill, 1986).
16. Shain, 1978, pp. 30–31.
17. Frankl, 1978, p. 39.
18. Wallis, p. 179.

Chapter 6

1. Kushner, 1986, p. 89.
2. Ibid., p. 97.
3. Gibran, pp. 29–30.
4. Shain, 1983, pp. 54–55.
5. Jacobi, p. 117.
6. Ibid., p. 118.
7. Gibran, p. 52–53.
8. Kushner, 1981, p. 111.
9. Petty, p. 46.

Chapter 7

1. Koestenbaum, 1981, pp. 11–12.
2. Miller, pp. 128–129.

Chapter 8

1. Abraham H. Maslow, *Toward a Psychology of Being* (New York: D. Van Nostrand Co., 1968), pp. 22–41.
2. Ibid., p. 155.
3. Ibid., p. 157.
4. Ibid., p. 141.
5. Ibid., p. 115.
6. Ibid., p. 46.
7. Ibid., p. 47.
8. Ibid., p. 164.
9. Ibid.
10. M. Scott Peck, *The Road Less Traveled* (New York: Simon & Schuster, 1978), p. 300.
11. Ibid., p. 273.
12. Maslow, p. 166.
13. Ibid., p. 210.
14. Abraham H. Maslow, *The Far Reaches of Human Nature* (New York: The Viking Press, 1971), p. 34.
15. Ibid., p. 36.
16. Ibid., p. 38.
17. Ibid., p. 39.
18. Denis Waitley and Rene L. Will, *The Joy of Working* (New York: Dodd, Mead & Co., 1985), pp. 57–58.
19. Wallis, p. 91.

Conclusion

1. Peck, p. 15.
2. Ibid., p. 16.
3. Kushner, 1981, pp. 146–147.

Bibliography

Bach, George R. *Pairing*. New York: Wyden, Inc., 1970.

Chesler, Phyllis. *Mothers on Trial*. New York: McGraw-Hill, 1986.

Caplan, Gerald. *An Approach to Community Mental Health*. New York: Grune and Stratton, 1961.

Erikson, Erik. *Childhood and Society*. New York: Norton & Co., 1963.

————. *Identity: Youth and Crisis*. New York: Norton and Co., 1968.

Frankl, Viktor. *Man's Search for Meaning*. New York: Washington Square Press, 1963.

————. *The Unheard Cry for Meaning*. New York: Simon & Schuster, 1978.

Gibran, Kahlil. *The Prophet*. New York: Alfred A. Knopf, 1985.

Group for the Advancement of Psychiatry. *The Educated Woman*. New York: Charles Scribners & Sons, 1975.

Jacobi, Jolande. *The Way of Individuation*. New York: New American Library, 1965.

Koestenbaum, Peter. *The Existential Crisis*. Campbell, Cal.: Institute for Clinical Philosophy, 1980.

————. *New Image of a Person*. Westport, Conn.: 1978.

————. *The Will to Freedom*. Campbell, Cal.: Institute for Clinical Philosophy, 1981.

Kübler-Ross, E. *On Death and Dying*. New York: Macmillan & Co., 1969.

Kushner, Harold S. *When All You've Ever Wanted Isn't Enough*. New York:L Summit Books, 1986.

————. *When Bad Things Happen to Good People*. New York: Schocken Books, 1981.

Lindbergh, Anne. M. *Hour of Gold, Hour of Lead*. New York: Mc Graw-Hill, 1971.

Maslow, Abraham H. *The Far Reaches of Human Nature*. New York: The Viking Press, 1971.

————. *Toward a Psychology of Being*. New York: D. Van Nostrand Co., 1968.

Miller, William. *Make Friends with Your Shadow*. Minneapolis: Augsburg Publishing, 1981.

Peck, M. Scott. *The Road Less Traveled*. New York: Simon & Schuster, 1978.

Petty, Jo. *Apples of Gold*. Norwalk, Conn.: C. R. Gibson Co.

Sanford, John A. *Evil: The Shadow Side of Reality*. New York: Crossroad, 1984.

Sheehy, Gail. *Pathfinders*. New York: William Morrow and Co. Inc., 1981.

Shain, Merle. *Hearts That We Broke Long Ago*. New York: Bantan Books, 1983.

————. *When Lovers Are Friends*. New York: J.B. Lippincott Co., 1978.

Veninga, Robert. *A Gift of Hope*. Boston: Little, Brown and Company, 1985.

Viorst, Judith. *Necessary Losses*. New York: Simon and Schuster, 1986.

Waitley, Denis. *The Seeds of Greatness*. New Jersey: Fleming H. Revel Co., 1983.

Waitley, Denis and Witt, Rene L. *The Joy of Working*. New York: Dodd, Mead & Co., 1985.

Wallis, Charles L. Editor. *Words of Life*. San Francisco: Harper & Row, 1966.